WISE
CRAFT
QUILTS

WISE
CRAFT
QUILTS

A Guide to Turning
Beloved Fabrics into
Meaningful Patchwork

BLAIR STOCKER

Foreword by
DENYSE SCHMIDT

Photographs by Stephanie Congdon Barnes

Roost Books
BOULDER
2017

Roost Books
an imprint of Shambhala Publications, Inc.
4720 Walnut Street
Boulder, Colorado 80301
roostbooks.com

9 8 7 6 5 4 3 2 1

First Edition
Printed in the United States of America
♾ This edition is printed on acid-free paper that
meets the American National Standards Institute
Z39.48 Standard.
♻ Shambhala Publications makes every effort
to print on recycled paper. For more information
please visit www.shambhala.com.

Distributed in the United States by Penguin Random House LLC and in Canada by Random House
of Canada Ltd

BOOK AND COVER DESIGN BY SHUBHANI SARKAR

Library of Congress Cataloging-in-Publication Data

Names: Stocker, Blair, author. | Barnes, Stephanie
Congdon, 1970– photographer.
Title: Wise craft quilts: a guide to turning beloved
fabrics into meaningful patchwork / Blair Stocker;
foreword by Denyse Schmidt; photographs by
Stephanie Congdon Barnes.
Description: First edition. | Boulder: Roost Books,
an imprint of Shambhala Publications, Inc., [2017]
Identifiers: LCCN 2016012230
ISBN 9781611803488 (hardcover: alk. paper)
Subjects: LCSH: Patchwork quilts. | Patchwork—
Patterns. | Textile fabrics. | Textile waste—
Recycling.
Classification: LCC TT835 .S73167 2017 | DDC
746.46—dc23 LC record available at https://lccn
.loc.gov/2016012230

For every maker and reader
who has ever told me about
a special collection of fabric they
hope to someday make a quilt with.
That someday is today.

Contents

THE QUILTS

Foreword

by Denyse Schmidt

I met Blair years ago when she attended a workshop I was teaching at Pacific Northwest College of Art. Blair was a standout student. She was enthusiastic and fun, and eager to learn. She clearly had years of design and crafting experience, as well as a fabric stash after my own heart. Most interesting to me, however, was Blair's familiar, quiet confidence in her own aesthetic, her own creative point of view. I could see that Blair was someone who would make her own mark on the quilting and crafting scene in a big way.

The beautiful body of work that Blair has created since then (and that she continues to create) is impressive and imbued with her unique sense of style and vision. Her quilts in particular resonate clear and true, with a tone that straddles then and now, our collective history and the individual story. Blair seems to possess an innate sense of the narrative of objects and materials, and it manifests in work with personality and authenticity.

One aspect of Blair's process that I particularly love is how she presents her quilts with visual stories on her blog at wisecrafthandmade.com. Blair artfully assembles a collage of inspiration images that offer a way into her thinking, the story that this quilt and its materials conjured up: interiors where the quilt might live, the person who might sleep under it, and images that surprise us with a palette and mood. The tableau offers a peek into the workings of a wonderfully creative mind, and in so doing, helps us to see the objects in our lives in new ways.

I wish I could have had my hands on this book when I began making quilts. (Though I am glad to have it now!) Instead of steps to re-create a project in exacting detail, Blair offers techniques and solutions for working with a wide range of fabric types, strategies for puzzling together odd-shaped pieces and sizes, and tips to setting parameters that will make design decisions more manageable. In essence, everything you need to use the materials *you* have on hand, in any form and quantity. Anyone can provide yardage calculations for a particular quilt pattern, but Blair has a singular ability to give you the tools to invent your own quilt, one informed by whatever vintage scraps or articles of clothing you wish to combine into a new visual story.

Of the many valuable tips and lessons in this book, one of the most important Blair offers can be found in the introduction: "I wrote this book to give all of us permission to cut into that special fabric." With that sentence, Blair addresses a stumbling block that prevents many of us from beginning a new venture—the feeling that somehow we're not good enough, talented enough, or that we need "permission." We've never quilted before, so why do we think we can quilt? Just who do we think we are, anyway? When you understand that you are creating something uniquely your own—that there is no "right" or "wrong" way—you begin to see the possibilities all around you. You begin to see with an artist's eye, and instead of judging, your mind is free to make connections that lead to new discoveries.

Take *Racer*, for instance—what an amazing idea to sew racing numbers together to create a graphically stunning and witty quilt! Another of my favorites is *D'Orly*; those sweet handkerchiefs sewn together immediately transport you back in time. *Value* also struck a particular chord with me. I love the idea of using every single scrap of fabric—and of friends getting together to share their stashes, just as pioneering women did when fabric was scarce. You just know that in addition to sharing fabric (then and now), friends are also sharing advice, confidences, support, and strength. Quilting quite literally provides ties that bind.

I particularly love the thoughtfulness and compassion that went into the idea of *Sensory*. Out of force of habit, we all mindlessly jingle coins in our pocket, twirl our hair, or drum our fingers on a table often to relieve anxiety or boredom. For those suffering with dementia, however, the need for repetitive motion is acute. *Sensory* is a beautiful quilt that provides comfort, warmth, and little thingamajigs sewn in expressly for fidgeting! Genius.

I'm so glad you've bought this book. Be sure to post pictures on social media, because I'll be wondering what unique ideas it will inspire in you!

Introduction

SEWING STORIES

Every patchwork quilt begins with fabric. And to me, quilts pieced from fabrics and remnants that have been saved, collected, shared, or acquired second-hand have a sparkle and uniqueness that simply cannot be made from new. Cherished fabrics and patchwork patterns that have lived previous lives have a bigger story to tell—the narrative they create has always intrigued me. Every quilt I encounter makes me curious: How did these fabrics all come together in this quilt? Was it a quilt made for necessity, to keep loved ones warm? Was it made to experience the process of making? Carefully cut from special fabric meant to be celebrated? What tale is told in that quilt? My love of quilt making is tied to the stories embedded in cloth and thread. My favorite quilts are those that provide physical and metaphorical warmth.

I discovered all of this by chance. Sixteen years ago I made my very first quilt. I wanted to preserve my daughter's sweet baby clothes, and a patchwork quilt spoke to me. I had never made a quilt before, yet I was uninhibited by my lack of technical skill. I followed some very basic instructions torn from a magazine and cut simple squares from her outgrown clothes, nursery curtains, and bedding. As the quilt grew and took shape, I realized that not only was I marking my daughter's early days, I was also discovering something about myself: the medium of patchwork suited me perfectly. I was hooked.

Now, after years of making quilts with repurposed fabric, I truly believe in the ability fabric has to preserve our memories and tell our stories. A particular fabric can immediately transport us back to places that we loved and felt loved in. Even if we do not have the physical cloth from those days, the discovery of a similar print or fabric can create recollections just as strong. Unexpectedly, something we come across in our daily life can bring up a comforting memory we want to hold on to. Memories can be evoked in so many ways, and there are just as many creative ways to translate these memories into a quilt.

These special fabrics are the starting point for each of the projects in this book. Each chapter will take you through the inspiration for a collection of fabrics (what I describe as the "feature fabric" of each quilt). This book honors cherished fabric of all kinds: childhood clothes, favorite shirts, prints worn by the women in our lives we look up to, fabrics that inspire our memories, just to name a few. It also celebrates the utilitarian aspect of reusing what we may already have. Even the humblest fabrics from our past can inform our lives and tell our stories. People who follow my work often tell me that my class reminds them of a special collection of fabric they have, one that they hope to make a quilt from. I always ask, what are you waiting for? I wrote this book to give all of us permission to cut into that special fabric. The time to begin a new story with it is now.

Color and Design Notes

Through the projects in this book, I will show you how to be inspired, not inhibited, by the limits of your own special collection of fabric. Guiding you through my own, approachable quilt making process, in each chapter I will explain how that quilt project came to be, how I work with that type of fabric, and how to create patchwork that is accessible and beautiful. You may have different amounts of cherished fabric for your quilt than I do for mine. For that reason, most of these quilts are constructed in blocks, allowing you to add or subtract the amount of blocks, based on what you have available and the size quilt you want to make.

Using vintage and secondhand fabric makes a very fun design challenge for your quilt making. In most cases, the fabric you have is limited, and it may not be possible to go to the fabric store to buy more. Maybe it is not your favorite shade of blue. Don't let these types of limitations inhibit you. In each chapter I will discuss inspiration and simple design rules I made for myself when creating that quilt. I'll also share the particular design problems that arose with each quilt and the solutions I arrived at to make each work. And it does always work. My hope is that you'll feel inspired by your own fabric collections and empowered to tackle any design challenge those collections present.

I am endlessly inspired by color and take every advantage to play with it in my quilt designs. In my own wardrobe, I feel most comfortable in gray, black, and indigo. My quilts are where I am happiest playing with any and every kind of combination of colors that inspire me. I look for inspiration everywhere. Mail order catalogs, store windows, vintage Fair Isle sweaters, and faded wallpaper are just a few of the many ways I get inspired by color and design. If I feel

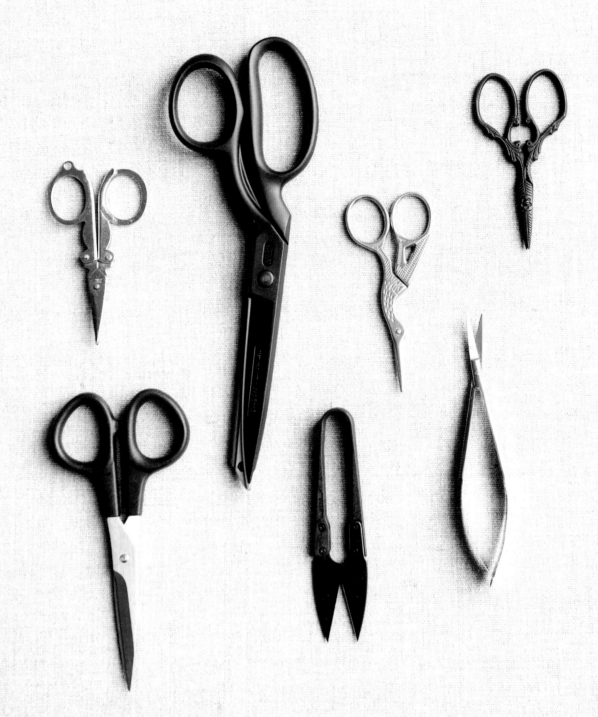

unsure about a color on its own, sometimes seeing it next to another color and feeling how those colors react together and inform each other can suddenly make the entire palette appear much more interesting. For example, the color red has never been a favorite of mine. Yet because I am really not sure why that is, I have challenged myself to use it and made several quilts with red as a focus. I realized through playing with red next to other colors that it could make sense in any design I create. Paired up with an orange or mustard yellow, suddenly it seems to work for me and can look so much more exciting! So I am going to give you a radical piece of advice. Forget color theory. Do not be tied to traditional rules about colors and how they work together. Think less about how colors should be used and more about how they create reactions in you. Work at developing and recognizing your own instinct for color and use it to discover what works together and speaks to you. Let your design process be intuitive. Open your mind to the possibility of what unlikely color groupings can do.

Explore your life through family stories, get inspiration for color and design techniques, pull together those fabrics you love, and enjoy the process of discovering your own style as a quilt maker.

How to Use This Book

Before getting starting, please take some time to read through Quilting 101 on page 145. This section goes over how to create a quilting tool kit of basic supplies that I will refer to in each of the chapters, as well as suggestions for preparing vintage fabrics, basic techniques for patchwork sewing, and methods for layering, quilting, binding, and finishing your quilts. All necessary templates can be found in the Templates section on page 158. They can also be printed directly from my website (wisecrafthandmade.com/templates).

I hope you find inspiration to begin your own special story with fabric and thread. Please share your quilts (both in progress and finished!) on your favorite social media outlets using the tag #wisecraftquiltsbook so we can see what you make.

WISE
CRAFT
QUILTS

JUL . 60

THE QUILTS

What I make with my hands,
I give of my heart.

—ANONYMOUS

1

Willy Loman

Although it is unclear what he actually *did* sell, the character of Mr. Loman from *Death of a Salesman* became a topic of conversation when a friend unearthed salesman sample cases dated from 1956 in the attic of his new home. Seven black carrying cases, to be exact, and they were full of swatch cards with fabrics on them, completely intact and untouched. The fabrics were for men's topcoats that could be "Tailored for a Custom Fit" by the Progress Company of Chicago, Illinois. Swatch card after swatch card had samples of woolens, woolen blends, sharkskin (yes!)—all the newest fabrics of the period. It seemed time had completely forgotten this collection and, in doing so, had graciously left them in impeccable condition. The swatches became a part of my stash, and I couldn't wait to use them.

The straightforward construction of *Willy Loman* will get you comfortable with piecing together squares and rectangles that are different sizes, and I will share my strategies for working with thicker fabrics such as wool or corduroy. But keep in mind, any type of fabric collection will work with this quilt design. The key is looking at the different possibilities within a limited color palette. Focus on creating surface interest with color and texture of the squares, which is the real heart of this design.

Maybe watch *Death of a Salesman* while you work. . . .

Finished Quilt Size:
49 × 56 inches,
for a crib- or lap-sized quilt

Techniques: General patchwork,
joining odd-sized pieces, sewing

with bulky fabrics, tying quilt
layers

Fabrics

For the Feature Fabric: 450 swatches. My swatches were a mixture of squares and rectangles, all sized a little differently, some were 3 × 3 inches, others were 4 × 5 inches.

For the Backing: 3⅝ yards quilting weight fabric. Backing should be least 4 inches larger than your quilt top's total length and width.

For the Binding: ½ yard of coordinating quilting weight fabric

Feature Fabric Suggestion: Swatches can be made from several pieces of clothing. Suitable fabrics are heavy cottons, wool or wool blends (like overcoats), upholstery fabric, and corduroy. The more variety in color and pattern you have, the better.

Other Materials

Low-Loft Cotton Batting: 1 package batting measuring at least 53 × 60 inches. Batting should be least 4 inches larger than your quilt top's total length and width.

1 skein of contrast worsted weight wool yarn for tying

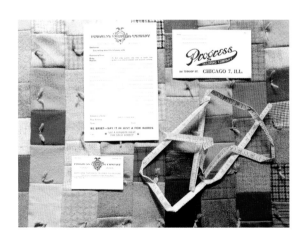

My Color and Design Notes

My quilt's size was dictated by the number of swatches I had, which was 450. Your quilt may need more or less, depending on the sizes of your cut pieces and desired quilt size. This design can easily be made larger or smaller depending on your materials and needs.

Due to the thickness of wool fabrics, I recommend sewing with a seam allowance closer to ½ inch instead of the standard ¼ inch. You also might find a sewing stiletto helpful to guide the thick layers of fabric under the presser foot.

Due to the thickness of the wool fabric, I pressed my seam allowances open to reduce overall bulk. If you use quilting cotton weight fabric, press all the seam allowances to one side.

Most of the swatches from the original cards were either dark or light—all typical colors you would imagine for men's overcoats. Once I started playing with the swatches on the design wall, I knew I wanted more color options to achieve the effect I had in mind: a gradual transition across the quilt from pale to dark. Given the limited palette of my swatches, this meant getting creative with how I could achieve more color and interest.

First, I added more texture and pattern options by using backs of some of the swatches. Next, a search on Etsy turned up some overdyed wool swatches in beautifully bright shades that I incorporated in the middle color range. Finally, I experimented with overdyeing some of the lighter swatches with Kool-Aid, creating some fun jewel tones that I sprinkled throughout the design. Decide how far you want to take your color palette and be open to experimenting.

For a few areas, I sewed two smaller scraps of fabric together to create one larger square or rectangle, then pieced them with the seam running perpendicular to the horizontal seams of the column in which they were included. I love this effect and think it really adds to the visual movement of the quilt. If you decide to try this, make sure there is good contrast between the two fabrics you piece together so the new patched piece shows up nicely in the design.

If two colors did not seem to work well next to each other, sometimes adding more color variations and contrast around them was all that I needed to make them work much better.

Rather than try to machine quilt the layers of a thick wool quilt such as this, I opted to hand tie the layers together using a periwinkle blue wool yarn. This added even more color contrast and texture to the quilt's surface. When the quilt is washed, the wool ties will felt and mat nicely, almost like a small pom-pom.

PREPARE THE FABRICS

1. Refer to the section Preparing Vintage and Secondhand Fabric (page 150) for information on preparing your fabric. I recommend washing the patchwork fabrics and backing all together to preshrink them (no need to wash the batting), unless you are worried about color bleeding, in which case you should wash separately until you are sure color bleeding will not be a problem. If you are using yardage for your swatches, wash and dry the entire piece first before cutting it into swatches. Once the fabrics are dry, steam press them well.

CUT AND SORT THE FABRICS

2. If you are starting with swatches as I did, you will simply work with the sizes you have. For cutting panels of clothing or remnants, use a rotary cutter, cutting mat, and long quilter's ruler to cut long 3-inch-wide strips from selvedge to selvedge. Sub cut these strips into squares and rectangles of varying widths.

3. Sort the cut pieces into 4 basic color groups: pale, medium, darker, and darkest. Decide which color ranges you would like more of. Maybe make a trip to the thrift store or experiment with overdyeing to fill in any sparse groups.

4. If you plan to over dye some of the fabric, do so now. To dye ¼ yard or less of prewashed wool or other natural fiber fabric with Kool-Aid, begin by presoaking the fabric to be dyed in warm water with a drop of Ivory Liquid soap for 45 minutes to 1 hour. Measure 8 cups of water into a pot and bring it to a boil, then turn the heat down to a simmer. Add 1 packet of Kool-Aid powder mix to the water and stir well. (Tip: You can deepen colors by adding more than one box of mix at a time.) Immerse the fabric and stir very well with tongs to evenly saturate the fabric. Simmer for 5 to 10 minutes, stirring often and checking periodically to see how much of the color is absorbed. When the color looks good and the water is clear or cloudy white, remove the fabric and immerse it in cool water to allow it to cool. Wash and dry the dyed fabric swatches thoroughly before using them in your quilt.

LAY OUT THE DESIGN

5. On a design wall, lay out the quilt design starting from the top, working down. To make a quilt similar to mine, you will need 19 vertical columns of swatches, and each column will be roughly 3 to 4 inches wide. Place the colors as if fitting together a puzzle, the paler fabrics start at the top, and the overall effect deepens as the eye moves toward the bottom of the quilt (see a). As the value deepens down each column, I found it fun to occasionally throw in a swatch of a much different value, but this is not necessary. Continue arranging the pieces, stopping occasionally to stand back and consider the full design layout from a distance. Use a reducing glass to take in the entire design and look at color distribution. Consider leaving the finished layout up overnight and look at it with fresh eyes in the morning. Once you are happy with the layout, take a picture to refer to later.

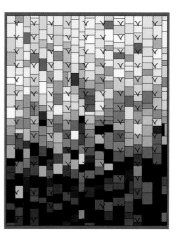

a.

b.

c.

CONSTRUCT THE QUILT TOP

6. Sew the columns together top to bottom, working from left to right across the quilt top. To keep things in order, take the swatches from the design wall 1 column at a time, always keeping the top swatch on top of the stack, then adding the rest of the swatches in order behind it. Bring the stack to the sewing machine, and sew each of the swatches together individually, right sides together, until the entire first column is done. Press the seam allowances open to reduce overall bulk. If your pieces are like mine, the sewn edges will not line up perfectly on both sides. Trim the uneven side of the finished column to even it up (see b). Place the sewn column back on the wall, grab the next one to sew, and repeat. Continue until all columns are sewn and trimmed.

7. Sew the columns to each other, starting from the left side of the layout. Pin 2 columns as needed, right sides together, and sew. Press the seam allowances open. The beauty of this design is that there are no seams to line up between the columns. Use a sewing stiletto to guide the bulkier areas under the presser foot if needed.

FINISH THE QUILT

Refer to Quilting 101 (page 145) for more information on each of these steps.

8. If needed, piece fabric together to make the quilt backing, which should measure at least 4 inches larger than the finished top's length and width. Layer the quilt backing, batting, and quilt top to create a quilt sandwich of all 3 layers. Pin baste the layers together.

9. Using a Frixion or water-soluble marker, measure and mark a grid of dots every 3 inches across the entire quilt top for tying.

10. Tie the quilt layers together with worsted wool yarn. Begin at the very center of the quilt top and work outward. Using a tapestry needle threaded with a long strand of yarn and working from the front of the quilt, make a stitch down and up through all layers at one of the marks, leaving tails at least 3 inches long (see c). Tie a square knot and evenly trim the yarn ends to the desired length. Repeat these knots across the entire quilt.

11. Once the ties are completed, trim the edges of all the quilt layers so they are even on all 4 sides, measuring 49 × 56 inches or your desired size.

12. Prepare the binding and bind the quilt following the instructions on page 154.

13. Label your quilt following the instructions on page 156.

2

Sample Box

I came across this collection of brocade upholstery showroom samples online, and it instantly reminded me of my great aunts. As a young girl, these women played big roles in my life, and I always felt loved by them. Each of their homes was adorned with a small and simple yet beautifully done parlor, and I remember them sitting together in these rooms, drinking black coffee, and prattling on about how to solve all the family's problems. I don't remember if there was brocade upholstery, but maybe there should have been.

These samples came together as a set, and are not a palette I usually work with. But I do love a creative challenge. To me, the final quilt feels very Bloomsbury, a British style from the early 1900s that embraced rich color and pattern, and exemplified filling your living space with things you love. I think this quilt would be so striking as a wall hanging or as a lap quilt draped over the back of a couch.

Finished Quilt Size:
44 × 44 inches,
for a throw-sized quilt

Finished Block Size:
9 × 9 inches

Techniques: General patchwork piecing, nine-patch piecing, walking foot quilting, making a quilt without binding

Fabrics

For the Feature Fabric: ½ yard each of 9 different fabrics

For the Backing: 3 yards quilting cotton. Backing should be least 4 inches larger than your quilt top's length and width.

Feature Fabric Suggestion: I used home decor weight, brocade upholstery samples for my quilt, nine color-ways of the same pattern. Four larger pieces measured 26 × 26 inches and 5 smaller pieces measured 17 × 17 inches. I suggest using as many colors as you can, re-peating colors for the larger squares only if you have to.

Other Materials

Low-Loft Cotton Batting: 1 package batting measuring at least 48 × 48 inches. Batting should be least 4 inches larger than your quilt top's length and width.

My Color and Design Notes

The color and style rules I impose on the quilts I make can be fun to play around with, and I suggest trying a few of your own rules as you lay out your quilt. While putting this layout up on my design wall, I made up a simple rule that the same colors would never sit side by side. My goal was to create good visual contrast between the nine patch blocks and the larger blocks. But, as usual, I followed this rule while it made sense and broke it when it didn't. At times, I preferred the way a small block of color looked next to a larger block of the same color. A trick I use to get more color options is to use both the right and wrong sides of the fabrics throughout the quilt top. Experiment with this in your own quilt; it can create some interesting color varia-tions.

This quilt does not have traditional binding; it just did not seem to work with the design. Some quilts simply work better without it. I will walk you through how to create a finished edge with no binding.

I machine quilted a simple straight line in a large dia-mond pattern across the solid squares of the quilt using a deep blue thread and my sewing machine's walking foot. These fabrics felt busy enough and didn't seem to need elaborate quilting.

PREPARE THE FABRICS

1. Refer to the section Preparing Vintage and Secondhand Fabric (page 150) for information on preparing your fabric. Knowing they had probably been han-dled frequently as showroom samples, I had my fabrics dry-cleaned before I cut them. Also knowing that this quilt would most likely be hung, the fabrics did not need to be put through a rigorous wash test. Each of my original pieces were chain stitched along the edges to prevent fraying. If fraying is a concern, trim the edges of your fabrics with pinking shears before washing or cleaning.

CUT THE FABRICS

2. Make the following cuts from your fabrics:

Thirteen squares measuring 9½ inches and 108 squares measuring 3½ inches. Cut each size square from as many different colors as you can.

LAY OUT THE DESIGN

3. On a design wall, lay out the quilt design starting from the top left, working across to the right, then down (see a). The Nine Patch blocks between each of the larger squares are created using 9 of the 3½-inch squares. Use 3 squares across and 3 down to create 1 Nine Patch block. I made each of my Nine Patch blocks very scrappy, randomly placing colors in each. You could play with alternating dark and light fabrics in your version, or play around with other color placement options, like creating a stripe effect by placing three darker ones in the center row, surrounded at top and bottom by lighter colors. Take a step back from the design often; considering it from a distance gives you a better idea of how the overall design is developing. When you are happy with the layout, take a picture to refer to as you begin construction.

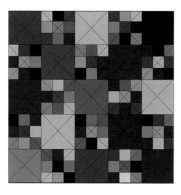

a.

CONSTRUCT THE QUILT TOP

4. Start by sewing the Nine Patch blocks. Take the squares for 1 Nine Patch block down from the design wall and position them in order by your sewing machine. With right sides together, start at the top left and stitch the first row of squares to each other; press the seam allowances to one side. Repeat for the next row, but press the seam allowances going in the opposite direction. Stitch the bottom row together and press the seam allowances in the same direction as the first row. From there, stitch the rows together, from top to bottom. By pressing the seam allowances of each row in opposite directions, the seams should now line up and nest when the rows are sewn together. Add a pin at this intersection, if you'd like, to ensure the seam allowances stay where you like when you sew the rows together; I use my sewing stiletto to act as a pin and hold it all together. Press the seam allowances to the same side. Check the size of each finished block and, if necessary, trim to measure 9½ inches square. Place the finished unit back on the design wall. Repeat this step to create a total of 12 Nine Patch blocks.

5. Sew the rows of the quilt together, starting from the top left, and going across, sewing the blocks together. Again, press each row's seam allowances in opposite directions so the seams will line up and nest when the rows are sewn together. Sew the rows to each other, press the seam allowances to the same side, and the quilt top is complete.

FINISH THE QUILT

Refer to Quilting 101 (page 145) for more information on each of these steps.

6. If needed, join fabric pieces together to make the appropriately sized quilt backing. Place your quilt backing on the worktable, wrong side up. Tape it to the table on all 4 sides with painter's blue tape to ensure it lies flat. Lay the batting over the backing. Instead of pin basting as I usually do, I found it helpful to use a bit of spray adhesive between the backing and batting to hold them together and flat (use in a well-ventilated area and follow package instructions). Once these layers are sandwiched together and smooth, remove the painter's tape and trim the batting and backing to be the same size as the quilt top; no need to leave extra for the next steps.

7. Turn these layers over, so the right side of the quilt backing is facing up. Lay the quilt top on top, right side down. Pin baste all 3 layers together, working from the center and moving out. Place the pins every 4 to 6 inches apart.

8. The 3 layers of this quilt are sewn together as a pillow. (Note: It is helpful to use a walking foot on your sewing machine for this step and the steps that fol-low.) Sew around the perimeter of all 4 sides using a ¼-inch seam allowance, leaving 10 inches unsewn along one edge for turning the quilt right side out. Backstitch at beginning and end. Once sewn, remove the basting pins, trim away any extra bulk at the corners, and turn the quilt right side out through the opening. Push the corner edges out carefully with a chopstick or closed pair of scissors if needed. Press the entire quilt well, and add basting pins through all layers every few inches to keep everything flat and in place for quilting. To finish the edges, topstitch along the edge of the quilt with a ¼-inch seam allowance, turning in and stitching the opening closed as you sew.

9. Using a ruler and a marking pen or painter's blue tape, mark diagonal lines going across the quilt, through the solid squares (see a). Mark diagonal lines going in the opposite direction, creating the diamond pattern. Quilt through all 3 layers on these lines, using your sewing machine's walking foot. Trim the loose threads.

10. Label your quilt following the instructions on page 156.

3

Baby

Baby clothes are especially hard to part with. Those first-year outfits, burp cloths, and receiving blankets are tied up with so many memories. This clothing makes up some of my favorite quilts because I love creating something so useable out of something that would most likely be stored away. I have made several baby clothes quilts since my first awkward try many years ago with my daughter's clothes; with experience I've developed some techniques and tricks along the way.

When given a pile of baby clothes to turn into a quilt, I take several things into consideration: the number of pieces I have to work with, colors, shapes, different fabric types, stains (sometimes those are fun to include), and special details like embroidery to incorporate. This basic block quilt design has areas large enough to show hints of the original garment and include special pieces or keepsakes yet small enough to incorporate most tiny-sized baby clothing. Sized for a twin bed, it will allow those first-year garments to keep the older child warm and comforted, with lots of individual blocks to inspire memories for the whole family.

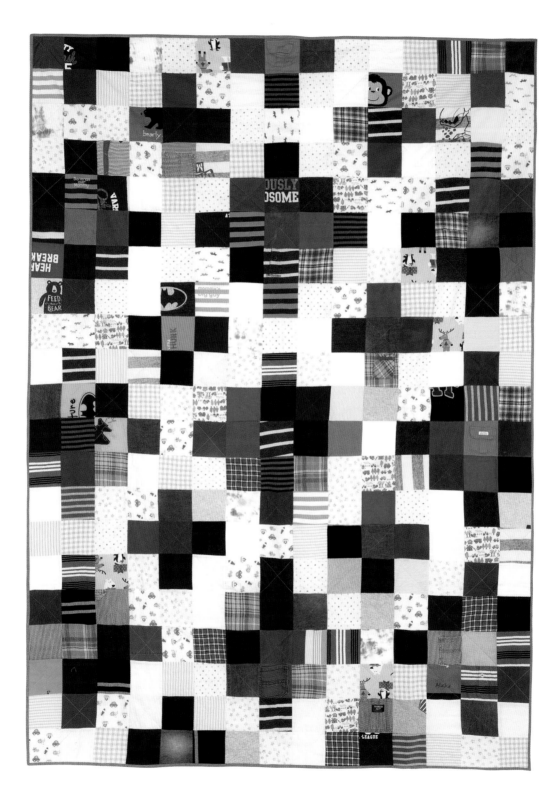

Finished Quilt Size:
63¾ × 89¼ inches,
for a twin-sized quilt

Finished Block Size:
4¼ × 4¼ inches

Techniques: Simple patchwork square construction, preparing unconventional fabrics for patchwork, creating design using color value, walking foot quilting

Fabrics

For the Feature Fabric: Assorted baby clothes. Knit and woven fabrics are both useable.

For the Quilt Top: In addition to the feature fabric, you will need ¾ yard 44-inch-wide quilter's cotton in a light color (use one color, such as cream or white, or several light-value fabrics) and ¾ yard 44-inch-wide quilter's cotton in a dark color (use one color, such as navy or dark green, or several dark-value fabrics).

For the Backing: 6 yards quilting cotton. The backing should be least 4 inches larger than your quilt top's total length and width.

For the Binding: ½ yard 44-inch-wide quilting cotton in a coordinating color

Feature Fabric Suggestion: It's difficult to give an exact number of clothing pieces you'll need, but keep in mind that the smallest baby outfits will only yield about 2 or 3 squares at the most. Err on the side of more clothing to start with. Consider also including receiving blankets, crib sheets, nursery curtains, anything that you wish to preserve. The more variety you have, the better. Don't think too much about color and pattern at this point. Clothing can be of any fabric, woven or knit, and any color.

Other Materials

3 packages (8 yards each) of ultra lightweight fusible interfacing (I used Pellon #12005096.)

Low-Loft Cotton Batting: 1 package batting measuring at least 67¾ × 93¼ inches. Batting should be least 4 inches larger than your quilt top's total length and width.

My Color and Design Notes

The overall design of this quilt begins by grouping all of the fabrics into either a light- or dark-value shade. It unifies the overall look of all the different shades, patterns, and colors of baby clothes yet still creates a quilt design that makes sense visually.

If there's not enough of a special fabric to make several squares, don't panic. Sew other pieces of fabric to it, and cut it to the correct block size.

I suggest adding in solid quilting cottons in both a dark and a light color to help further unify the design and bring cohesion to the many patterns and colors you will most likely be working with.

The steps for this quilt are best completed in batches. For example, I will spend an afternoon cutting the clothing apart, cutting away seams, and so on. I will then spend another chunk of time stabilizing all the knit pieces at the ironing board. (This is a great time to catch up on podcasts or watch a movie!)

Consider using both the front and the back of an interesting fabric for extra variety if needed. Just keep in mind you will need to decide if you'll do this before the stabilizing step.

It is great fun to incorporate tiny pockets, logos, snaps, and buttons, but leave choking hazards like these out if the quilt will be used for small child. You can save special things like buttons to sew on later.

When laying out this design, it is important keep a strong contrast at the areas where the color changes from light to dark, so that the pattern is clearly defined. For example, where one dark section ends, be sure to use a clearly light-valued fabric beside it, instead of one that could read light or dark, so that the pattern shows up nicely.

PREPARE THE FABRICS

1. Refer to the section Preparing Vintage and Secondhand Fabric on page 150 for information on preparing your fabric. Once everything is clean, cut the clothing into fabric panels, cutting close to the seams in order to remove them and get the most fabric out of each outfit. I cut most away but actually left a few seams in for interest.

2. Most infant clothing is made of knit fabric—comfortable for baby but not ideal for patchwork. To remove the stretch and make it suitable for patchwork, knit fabric needs to be stabilized. Following the manufacturer's instructions, cut a piece of interfacing roughly the size of the fabric piece (maybe slightly smaller so you won't fuse the piece to your ironing board). At your ironing board, place it glue side down onto the back of the fabric. Cover everything with a press cloth and iron it to fuse the interfacing to the back of each piece of knit fabric. This is a tedious step but very necessary. (I have been known to pay teenagers to do this for me; money makes them suddenly very helpful.)

3. Sort the fabric panels into 2 piles: 1 light value and 1 dark value. If there are any shades that seem to fall in the middle, you can set them aside initially, but don't take too much time considering the value shade of any one fabric. Each will naturally fall into one of the values as the design is laid out.

4. Cut as many 4¾-inch squares as you can get from each of the fabric panels; you will need 130 dark squares and 125 light squares. From the solid quilting cottons, cut thirty 4¾-inch light squares and thirty 4¾-inch dark squares. You will need a total of 160 dark squares and 155 light squares, for a total of 315 squares.

LAY OUT THE DESIGN

5. On a design wall, lay out the quilt design starting from the top left, working across and down. Alternate between the light- and dark-value fabrics to create diamond-shaped patterns evenly across the quilt (see a). If the design is feeling visually cluttered, this is where adding in the light and dark solid squares can help. I find this is definitely a pattern that is good to take a break from or look at through a reducing glass before you finalize it. The pattern needs to be

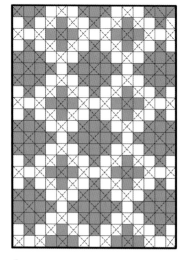

a.

clearly visible, so take your time. When you are happy with the layout, take a picture to refer to as you begin construction.

CONSTRUCT THE QUILT TOP

6. Starting at the top and working in rows from left to right down the quilt, remove the first row of squares from the design wall and sew them together. Repeat this step with each row, putting it back up on the design wall once sewn. Press each row's seam allowances to the opposite side to nest the seams when the rows are sewn together.

7. Sew the rows to each other, from top to bottom, nesting the seams to line them up. Press all seam allowances to one consistent side.

FINISH THE QUILT

Refer to Quilting 101 (page 145) for more information on each of these steps.

8. If needed, piece fabric together to make the quilt backing, which should measure at least 4 inches larger than the finished top's length and width. Layer the quilt backing, batting, and quilt top to create a quilt sandwich of all 3 layers. Pin baste the layers together.

9. The layers of this quilt are a bit bulky, so I suggest simple walking foot quilting. Using a ruler and a marking pen or painter's blue tape, mark diagonal lines going through the squares from the top of one corner to the bottom opposite corner, creating a diamond pattern (see a). Quilt through all 3 layers on these lines, using your sewing machine's walking foot. Trim the loose threads. Skip over any areas with pockets as you stitch so they can still be used.

10. Once the quilting is complete, trim the edges of all the quilt layers to be even on all 4 sides, measuring 63¾ × 89¼ inches or your desired size.

11. Prepare the binding and bind the quilt following the instructions on page 154.

12. Label your quilt following the instructions on page 156.

4

Indigo

Denim is always a favorite material to use in my quilts, perhaps because I worked as a denim designer once. I am fascinated by the absolute love and devotion a person can feel toward his or her favorite pair of jeans, as well as all the endless variations of the cloth itself. In quilts, like in our wardrobes, jeans go with just about anything. In our house, if a pair falls out of favor, they land on my fabric shelves. Everybody looks for their own clothing contribution in the finished quilts I make with them. And the denim continues to work hard at keeping us warm and protected, long after its usefulness as clothing has passed.

Denim can be a thick fabric for quilt making, and I've included all my favorite tips to work this fabric into the classic Delectable Mountains block pattern for this project.

Finished Quilt Size:
50 × 54 inches,
for a throw-sized quilt

Finished Block Size:
5 × 9 inches

Techniques: Sewing with bulky
fabrics, creating half-square
triangle and Delectable Mountain
blocks, tying quilt layers

Fabrics

For the Feature Fabric: Denim clothing in a variety of
shades

For the Backing: 3½ yards quilting cotton. Backing
should be least 4 inches larger than your quilt top's total
length and width.

For the Binding: ½ yard 44-inch-wide quilting cotton
in a coordinating color

Feature Fabric Suggestion: Cast-off jeans from your
family are the perfect place to start. Grab more from the
thrift store if you need to or decide you'd like to include
additional finishes (go for the larger, inexpensive pieces, which will yield more fabric). As a general guideline,
one pair of adult women's denim jeans will yield approximately sixteen 6⅜ × 6⅜-inch squares. This, of course,
can vary greatly depending on size, fit, cut, and so on.

Other Materials

Low-Loft Cotton Batting: 1 package twin-sized batting. Batting should be least 4 inches larger than your
quilt top's total length and width.

1 skein of worsted weight wool yarn in a coordinating
color

My Color and Design Notes

I didn't use any
special stitching or
trim details from
my denim pieces
because there are
a lot of seams in
this quilt. If you'd
like to use details
like seams, pockets, and patches (and you definitely
should!), consider one of the other patterns in the book
with fewer seams (such as Baby, page 17), so the details can really stand out.

Denim is another fabric where both the back and the
front can offer completely different color options. Also,
stains? A small rip or frayed area? Consider incorporating them into the design. Once I had all my denim
pieces, I separated them into dark and light piles.
Playing with denim shades this way will unify the design,
as well as add interest and movement. If the denim has
Lycra in it, or stretch, don't pull at the fabric too much
when sewing.

Iron all the seam allowances open to help distribute the
bulk on the underside of the quilt top. Use a cotton setting and lots of steam. If you find the beginning or end of
the seam pulling apart, backstitching will prevent this.

PREPARE THE FABRICS

1. Refer to the section Preparing Vintage and Secondhand Fabric on page
150 for information on preparing your fabric. Once everything is clean, use
fabric scissors to cut off the legs and open them up at their side seams. Cut
away all thick seams and bulky areas.

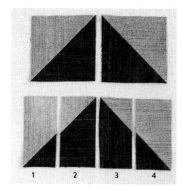

a.

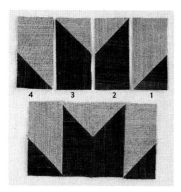

b.

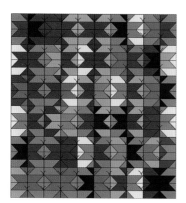

c.

CUT AND SORT THE FABRIC

2. Cut as many 6⅜-inch squares as you can get from each of the legs. You will need a total of 60 light-valued squares and 60 dark-valued squares. (Note: If there are any shades that seem to fall in the middle, you can set them aside initially. They will naturally fall into one of the values as the design is laid out.)

MAKE HALF-SQUARE TRIANGLES

3. Pair the light squares with the dark squares to create 60 pairs. Be sure you have good contrast within each pair (but for variety, you could also break this rule and pair a couple of similar shades together—just sayin'). Place each pair right sides together. With a Frixion pen or a pencil, draw a diagonal line across the wrong side of the lighter square, from the top of one corner to the bottom opposite corner. Repeat this step with all the squares.

4. At the sewing machine, stitch each pair together, ¼ inch away from the line you drew, on both sides of the line. (Tip: I like to chain piece these squares by feeding the pairs through the machine one after the other without cutting the thread. I sew along one side of the line on all the pairs first, then feed the pairs through again to sew on the other side of the line.) Once all the pairs are sewn, cut each pair in half on the drawn line but keep the pairs together. Press the seam allowances open, and square up the resulting 2 squares (which are now half-square triangles) to measure 5½ × 5½ inches.

MAKE THE DELECTABLE MOUNTAIN BLOCKS

5. Position a matching pair of half-square triangles on your worktable, side by side. The left block should have the diagonal seam line going up on the right side, with the darker fabric on the bottom half of the square; the right block should have the diagonal seam line going up on the left, also with the darker fabric on the bottom (see a). Using a rotary cutter and ruler, cut each block down the middle, widthwise, creating two 2¾ × 5½-inch units from each square. The squares going left to right (1, 2, 3, 4) should be repositioned in reverse order (4, 3, 2, 1) (see b). Sew these strips together in this order. Press the seam allowances open. Each pair makes one Delectable Mountain block. Check that the block measures 5½ × 9½ inches and square up if needed. Repeat for all the half-square pairs, for a total of 60 blocks.

LAY OUT THE DESIGN

6. On a design wall, lay out the quilt design starting from the top left, working across and down, following the layout and block orientation in the illustration (see c). You will have 6 rows of 10 blocks each. It can be helpful to look at the overall design through a reducing glass to ensure that the different indigo shades are well distributed across the quilt. There really is no wrong way to distribute indigo shades, but it is fun to play around with mixing the different variations around the quilt top. (I intentionally turned one of my blocks facing a different way. Maybe you can spot it.) When you are happy with the layout, take a picture to refer to later.

CONSTRUCT THE QUILT TOP

7. Starting at the top and working in rows from left to right, remove the first row of blocks from the design wall and sew them together. Add a pin where seams align as needed. Press the seam allowances open. Put the finished row back on the design wall, grab the next row, and repeat until all the rows are sewn.

8. Sew the rows to each other, from top to bottom, pressing seam allowances open.

FINISH THE QUILT

Refer to Quilting 101 (page 145) for more information on each of these steps.

9. If needed, piece fabric together to make the quilt backing, which should measure at least 4 inches larger than the finished top's length and width. Layer the quilt backing, batting, and quilt top to create a quilt sandwich of all 3 layers. Pin baste the layers together.

10. Quilt the layers together by tying them with the yarn. If you tie at every seam that creates a diamond shape, as I did, there is no need to mark the quilt top before tying (see c). Begin in the center of the quilt top and work outward for this step. Using a tapestry needle threaded with a long strand of yarn and working from the front of the quilt, make a stitch down and up through all layers at one of the marks, leaving tails at least 3 inches long. Tie a square knot and evenly trim the yarn ends to the desired length. Repeat this step across the entire quilt.

11. Once the ties are complete, trim the edges of all the quilt layers to measure 50 × 54 inches, or your desired size.

12. Prepare the binding and bind the quilt following the instructions on page 154.

13. Label your quilt following the instructions on page 156.

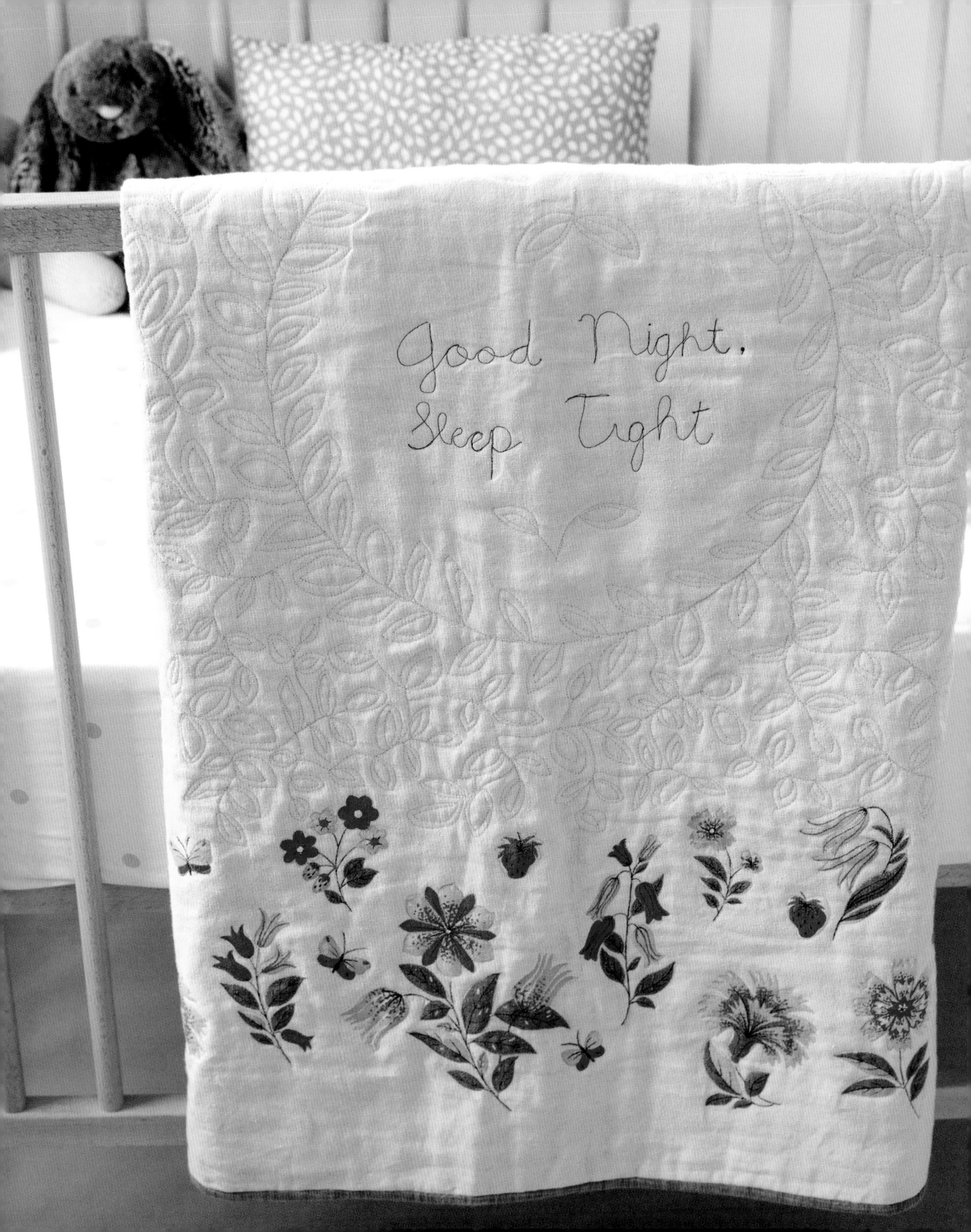
Good Night,
Sleep Tight

5

Whole Cloth

I have collected many table linens over the years and am drawn to the sense of home and comfort they represent to me. My grandmothers always used tablecloths for family dinners. They were not handmade and did not have any special meaning that I remember, but to me they meant home. Maybe that is why I am still so fond of them, even though I rarely use a tablecloth in my own home.

Creating an entire quilt top out of a single piece of fabric is a great way to make a quilt quickly, and if the cloth you are using has special meaning, it is even better. A vintage linen breakfast tablecloth inspired my quilt, and it turned out to be the ideal size for a baby's crib. Cheerful flowers and vines fill the perimeter of the cloth, leaving the center area completely open—the perfect place to hand or machine embroider a simple message.

Is there anything cozier than a baby snuggled in a handmade quilt?

Finished Quilt Size:
47 × 59 inches,
for a crib-sized quilt

Techniques: Creating a quilt top
from whole cloth, free motion
quilting, using templates

Fabrics

For the Feature Fabric: Linen or cotton tablecloth measuring 48 × 60 inches

For the Backing: 3¾ yards quilting cotton. Backing should be least 4 inches larger than your quilt top's total length and width.

For the Binding: ½ yard 44-inch-wide quilting cotton in a coordinating color

Feature Fabric Suggestion: A linen tablecloth is perfect for this project because it is such a beautiful, strong, and durable natural fabric. Other suitable fabrics are cotton or lightweight wool.

If you would like to try free motion quilting on this project, as I did, look for tablecloths that aren't too busy and have patterning that can be easily outlined with free motion stitching. You can also do hand embroidery instead if you prefer. If you do pick a tablecloth with a more intricate pattern, you can choose to only outline certain areas in the design.

Other Materials

Template for words in the center of the quilt, page 158

Tracing Paper (I used Saral wax-free tracing paper.)

Printer

Low-Loft Cotton Batting: 1 package twin-sized batting cut to size. Batting should be least 4 inches larger than your quilt top's total length and width.

My Color and Design Notes

You can easily create your own message for the center of the quilt using a word processing program on your computer, allowing you to personalize it to the baby's name, birth date, or other message.

The print on my tablecloth inspired the way I quilted it. I used free motion embroidery on my home machine to outline all the flowers and vines, and I continued stitching simple vines into the empty space around the center motif. (Read more about setting your machine up for free motion quilting on page 153.) I encourage you to try it, very fun!

Normally when I free motion quilt, I use the same color in the top and bobbin thread, but I made an exception for this quilt. I wanted the overall design to be calming, so I matched the bobbin thread to the backing fabric. I suggest testing the tension settings on a scrap piece before proceeding to stitch on the quilt to be sure there is no bobbin thread pulling up to the front of the quilt and vice versa.

I used a contrast sewing thread to free motion stitch "Good Night, Sleep Tight" to allow it to show up.

If the idea of free motion stitching this quilt feels like too much, it would look equally beautiful to hand embroider around the motifs.

Do not shy away from a little stain or two. Follow my advice in Preparing Vintage and Secondhand Fabric (page 150) to remove as much as you can. From there, if there is anything unsightly, you can appliqué small patches of meaningful fabrics over it (see *Boro*, page 41).

PREPARE THE FABRIC

1. Refer to the section Preparing Vintage and Secondhand Fabric on page 150 for information on preparing your fabric. Press the tablecloth well, using a smoothing product like Flatter to help get the wrinkles out. Fold the cloth in quarters and lightly crease at the folds to mark the center.

PREPARE THE DESIGN MOTIFS FOR THE QUILT TOP

2. It is best to mark the free motion quilting design directly on the quilt top before sandwiching the layers together. Print out the "Good Night, Sleep Tight" template at full size (page 158). Fold the template in quarters to find and mark the center of the motif. Match up the folds of the template and the tablecloth to center the design on the front of the tablecloth. Pin the template in place.

3. Place a sheet of tracing paper underneath the template, and using a pencil, trace the entire design onto the tablecloth. Remove the template and tracing paper.

4. If your tablecloth fabric is printed with motifs, plan to free motion quilt or hand quilt around them, and these do not need to be marked first. If your cloth has a large blank space, as mine did, use a Frixion or water-soluble marking pen to draw other motifs on the front of the cloth (around the central motif) that will also be stitched. These stitches are needed to hold the quilt layers together as well as add detail and textures to the quilt surface.

FINISH THE QUILT

Refer to Quilting 101 (page 145) for more information on each of these steps.

5. Piece fabric together to make the quilt backing, which should measure at least 4 inches larger than the finished top's length and width. Layer the quilt backing, batting, and quilt top to create a quilt sandwich of all 3 layers. Pin baste the layers together. (Note: My linen tablecloth was a bit heavy and slippery, and using a bit of temporary fabric adhesive spray between the layers helped to hold everything together smoothly.)

a.

6. Quilt the layers. Start at the center of the quilt and work outward. With the free motion foot and a contrasting thread, start by stitching the words in the center of the quilt. Switch to matching top thread next, and stitch over the designs drawn on the tablecloth. Last, stitch around all the printed designs along the perimeter of the quilt (see a).

7. When the quilting is complete, cut off any hemmed edges of the tablecloth and trim the edges of all the quilt layers to be even on all 4 sides, measuring 47 × 59 inches or your desired size.

8. Prepare the binding and bind the quilt following the instructions on page 154.

9. Label your quilt following the instructions on page 156.

6

Racer

I have my husband, Peter, to thank for this quilt—both for his suggestion of it as well as for the years of bike racing that produced the stack of Tyvek race numbers I had to work with. Tyvek is a synthetic, lightweight, durable material that acts a lot like paper but is, in fact, much stronger, and even washable. Cyclists, runners, and marathoners often hang on to their race numbers after the event is over, and this is a unique way to actually reuse them. This picnic-style quilt makes a functional way to sit in the grass and enjoy watching future races. Roll it up, use the ties to secure it, and keep it in the car.

Finished Quilt Size:
40 × 45 inches,
for a picnic-sized quilt

Techniques: Sewing with unconventional fabrics, improvisational patchwork piecing, free motion quilting, adding ties to binding

Fabrics

For the Feature Fabric: 35 Tyvek or fabric race numbers

For the Backing: 3 yards 44-inch-wide quilting cotton. Backing should be least 4 inches larger than your quilt top's total length and width.

For the Binding and Ties: 1 yard 44-inch-wide quilting cotton in a coordinating color

Feature Fabric Suggestions: Be sure that your race numbers are Tyvek or some sort of fabric, as paper or cardboard ones will not work. The race numbers will likely be all different sizes, as mine were.

Other Materials

Low-Loft Cotton Batting: 1 package crib-sized batting cut to size. Batting should be least 4 inches larger than your quilt top's total length and width.

Binder or bulldog clips (to use instead of pins)

My Color and Design Notes

Instead of pinning the pieces together to sew, I used binder clips. The holes from the pins may not go away.

Start with a fresh needle in your machine for this project. One designated for leather or denim will punch through the Tyvek nicely (I used Schmetz 100/16 Jeans needle).

Finger pressing the seam allowances to one side, rather than using an iron, works well for this project. If you need to use the iron for any reason, test the iron on the lowest heat setting to be sure it doesn't damage the Tyvek and adjust the heat from there.

If you have never tried free motion quilting before, this is a perfect first project. The construction and layout for this quilt is very much like *Willy Loman* (page 3). Reading through that project may provide additional tips.

As I considered the overall design of my quilt, it felt more interesting to play with the orientation of the numbers and have some facing different directions. I even cut off part of some. Don't feel compelled to keep every inch of each number. The memory is there, even if you only see a portion of it in the final piece.

This design really has no top or bottom. My feeling was that it would be directly sat upon, and each part of the design could be the focus, all on its own, at any time.

If you use the finished quilt on wet grass, turn the number side face down for the best protection. Otherwise, both sides are useable.

PREPARE THE FABRICS

1. Refer to the section Preparing Vintage and Secondhand Fabric on page 150 for information on preparing your fabric. I washed the numbers together in a regular washing cycle and low heat dryer setting, which cleaned them and softened them up a bit as well.

LAY OUT THE DESIGN

2. On a design wall, lay out the quilt design starting from the top, working down, taping each number in place with painter's blue tape. To make a quilt similar to mine, you will need 6 vertical columns of numbers, each with 6 or 7 numbers, depending on their size (see a). Piece smaller, odd-sized numbers together to make one bigger piece as needed. Once you are happy with the layout, take a picture to refer to as you begin construction.

a.

CONSTRUCT THE QUILT TOP

3. Sew the columns together top to bottom, working from left to right across the quilt top. To keep things in order, I took the numbers from the design wall one column at a time. Sew each of the numbers together one at a time, right sides together, until the entire first column is done. Finger press the seam allowances to one side. If the sewn edges don't line up perfectly on both long sides of the column, trim the uneven edge to straighten. Tape the sewn column back on the wall, grab the next one to sew, and repeat. Continuing until all columns are sewn and trimmed.

4. Sew the columns together, starting from the left side. Use binder clips to hold the columns wrong sides together as needed and sew. Finger press the seam allowances to one side.

FINISH THE QUILT

Refer to Quilting 101 (page 145) for more information on each of these steps.

5. Piece fabric together to make the quilt backing, which should measure at least 4 inches larger than the finished top's length and width. Layer the quilt backing, batting, and quilt top to create a quilt sandwich of all 3 layers. Instead of pinning, I suggest using a spray baste between the layers to hold them together. (Note: For extra stability, I also added some binder clips around the edges when I was quilting close to them.)

6. Quilt the layers using free motion embroidery, following the instructions on page 153. I stitched loosely around each of the numbers with coordinating thread. Tip: There is no need to cut your thread each time you move the needle in position to sew around a new number. When you reach the last stitches of one number, take a few teeny tiny stitches in place to secure your thread, bring the needle up, raise the presser foot up, position the next number under your

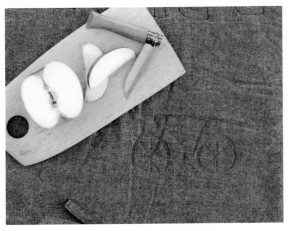

b.

presser foot, and lower the foot, all without cutting your thread. Take a few small stitches to secure, and begin free motion stitching again. Once you're done go back and trim these "jump stitches" on both the front and back of the quilt.

7. I also "drew" a bicycle on one corner in contrasting red thread (see b). I did an Internet search for a simple bike drawing, and referenced that image to draw a bike directly on the quilt using a Frixion pen. I free motion stitched over each of the lines a few times to add emphasis to the image, starting and ending my stitches by making tiny stitches like I did around the numbers.

8. Make the ties. With the same fabric you plan to use for binding, cut 2 strips 2½ × 44 inches. At the ironing board, press each strip in half lengthwise, wrong sides together. Open up the fold and bring each of the cut edges to meet at the press line. Press the strips again. Fold the entire strap in half lengthwise again, and press. Sew around all 4 sides of each strip, close to the edge. (Note: I used a contrast thread.)

9. Attach the ties to the quilt. Find the center of one of the shorter sides of the quilt. Measure 10 inches away from either side of the center and mark. Fold each tie in half lengthwise, and place one strap at each of the marks, with the fold aligned with the edge of the quilt and ends of the tie toward the quilt's center. Stitch in place to secure the tie, staying close to the quilt's edge (the tie will be secured further when the binding is sewn on).

10. Prepare the binding and bind the quilt following the instructions on page 154. I found it very helpful to baste around all 4 sides of this quilt, a scant ¼ inch from the edge, before attaching the binding, using a long basting stitch and a walking foot (you could also use a patchwork foot). Once the binding is completely sewn onto the quilt, using a hand-sewing needle, make a few stitches at the straps to secure them to the outside of the binding, away from the quilt.

11. Label your quilt following the instructions on page 156.

7

Boro

Boro is a Japanese term that means "tattered cloth" or "rags." It represents the patched, hand stitched, make-do tradition of mending cloth in Japan. Boro cloths are a beautiful example of creative reuse. Once defined as "folk fabric" and viewed as the poor man's solution to mending worn clothing, today it is valued for its unique handmade beauty and functionality. Decorative hand stitches called *sashiko* (pronounced SA-shee-ko) reinforce the fabric and further enhance the surface of the cloth. These stiches are added over time, all contributing more character to Boro.

I used a collection of vintage Japanese hand-dyed indigo and cotton rice sack cloths for my own *Boro*. This method of literally making cloth from rags can be used to create a larger cloth from small scraps of coveted fabrics. I chose not to use any batting inside this project (it only has a center layer of muslin), creating something that can be used as a wall hanging. It could also be pulled out and used as a summer coverlet. The weight is perfect for warmer months when a heavy quilt would be too much.

Finished Quilt Size:
60 × 52 inches, for a
wall hanging or throw-sized quilt

Techniques: Improvisational
piecing, making a lighter weight
coverlet without traditional
batting, decorative hand stitching,
hand quilting

Fabrics

For the Feature Fabric: Large pieces of indigo or similar dark blue fabric for the base (these pieces will need to measure 64 × 56 inches in total when sewn together); assorted sizes of prized fabric scraps and remnants for creating patches on the surface

For the Backing and Center: Two 64 × 56-inch pieces of quilter's muslin

Other Materials

Perle cotton thread, embroidery floss, crochet cotton, or sashiko thread in an assortment of coordinating and contrasting colors

My Color and Design Notes

This coverlet is not about precision piecing or fussy seams, which is what I love about it. Think of it purely as a base cloth for learning decorative hand stitches and collecting your favorite scraps to be pulled out whenever the inspiration strikes. My *Boro* folded up neatly, and I carried it with me, allowing me to spend a few minutes stitching while waiting for kids, watching a movie, or having coffee with a friend.

When planning the look of this project, I wanted the overall palette to be dark indigo and cream. Finding a vintage cotton rice sack with bright pink printing on eBay was a happy accident that inspired the accents of bright pink hand stitching I added later. When the rice sack arrived in the mail, I remembered another small handkerchief in my fabric stash that had pink edge stitching. I love projects that evolve like this. Be open to allowing one initial idea to develop in unexpected ways.

Do not overthink or fret over whether your fabrics go together or not. Keep your palette simple, trust your intuition, and make decisions based on instinct. You will be pleasantly surprised at how beautifully the fabrics blend when you join them with your hand stitches.

Pieces that are not uniform in size are what make this design interesting; do not go for symmetry. Have fun with it. You are the designer.

I chose a few different shades of pink thread and one or two small contrasting color scraps, like the pea green, to add some visual contrast to the deep indigo blues that dominate this coverlet. A little contrast goes a long way. Audition a few colors, but ultimately choose only one or two, and keep the rest of the stitching in a complementary color family. Otherwise, the striking effect of the contrasting stitches scattered across the quilt becomes too busy. Sashiko stitching is subtle and geometric, beautiful all on its own as a simple design element.

I used a hera marker to mark the long vertical quilting guidelines instead of a marking pen. The crease made by this little tool is permanent but subtle, allowing you to mark lines that don't need to be stitched right away. (Read more about marking your quilt in Quilting 101, page 145.)

PREPARE THE FABRICS

1. Refer to the section Preparing Vintage and Secondhand Fabric on page 150 for information on preparing your fabric. Prewash all the fabrics together. Consider using a color catcher in the wash load to absorb any indigo dye in the water if that is a concern. Dry and press.

LAY OUT AND PIECE THE BACKGROUND

2. Larger pieces of fabric will be sewn together to create the base of *Boro*, and the smaller swatches will be sewn over these. Creating this base is a very free-form process. I started with a favorite fabric for the center of the quilt and put that in the center area of the design wall. Next, I added other fabrics around that, one piece at a time. This improvisational piecing method is all about placing a few fabrics around the center, stepping back and looking at the design, perhaps sewing pieces together that seem to be working together, trimming their edges to even them up, adding a new fabric, and so on. Press the seam allowances open to reduce bulk and allow for easier hand stitching. Once all the larger pieces are sewn together, trim the sides of the quilt if necessary to square up the edges. (This is similar to how the *Tagged* quilt is constructed, page 117.)

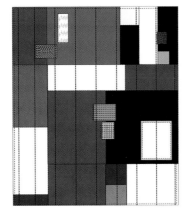

a.

ADD THE PATCHES

3. Keeping the larger base layer on your design wall (pinning if necessary to hold the weight), begin pinning the smaller patches onto the base cloth. This allows you to stand back and consider the whole design as you add new pieces. Press patches before adding them, cut down any that seem too big. Think of where textiles might have a naturally worn area, like seam joins, and consider adding scraps there. Stand back to look at the overall design often and notice how the colors work together. Put some music on and get inspired! Refer to the layout of my quilt to get a sense of my proportions and composition (see a). Take a photo of the top once you have all the pieces pinned on and are happy with the layout.

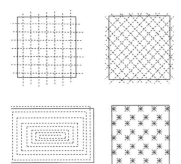

b.

4. Sew the smaller patches to the base cloth. I used a neutral thread to machine stitch around the swatches to secure them before adding hand stitching. This is an optional step, but it makes the entire project more portable if you plan to hand stitch on the go. Use a ruler and a fabric marking pen to draw gridlines directly on the patch and plan to extend this stitching on to the background fabric to help secure it (see b). With a length of Perle cotton or cotton embroidery thread, begin stitching each swatch to the base layer; use my *Boro* as a guide or make your own simple designs. I stitched simple grid patterns, a series of square shapes, and diamond patterns. Do this for all the patches on the coverlet, varying the embroidery thread colors and stitch patterns to add interest (see c). Complete all the hand stitching before continuing to the next step.

c.

FINISH THE QUILT

Refer to Quilting 101 (page 145) for more information on each of these steps.

5. Make the quilt backing and sandwich the layers of your quilt. This step is constructed similarly to *Sample Box* (page 11). Join lengths of muslin together to make a quilt backing that measures 64 × 56 inches or 4 inches larger than your quilt top's length and width. Make another identical piece to use for the inside layer instead of batting. Lay the backing on your worktable, wrong side up, and tape it down to the table on all 4 sides with painter's blue tape to ensure it lies flat. Lay the second piece of muslin directly over the backing. Instead of pin basting, I used a bit of spray adhesive between the layers of muslin to hold them together and flat (use in a well-ventilated area and follow the manufacturer's instructions). Untape and turn these layers over, so the backing is facing up. Lay the coverlet top over the backing muslin, right sides together. Pin baste the layers together. (There's no need to completely pin baste for this step, just place pins randomly around to hold the layers in place.) Once all the layers are secured together, trim the layers of all 4 sides to be even.

6. Sew the layers of the coverlet. The 3 layers of this quilt are sewn together as a pillow. Sew around the perimeter of all 4 sides using a ¼-inch seam allowance, leaving 10 inches unsewn along one edge for turning the quilt. Once the quilt is sewn, remove the basting pins, trim away any extra bulk at the corners, and turn the quilt right side out through the opening. Push the corner edges out carefully with a chopstick or closed pair of scissors if needed. Press the entire quilt, and add basting pins every few inches to keep everything flat and in place for quilting. To finish the edges, topstitch along the edge of the quilt with a ¼-inch seam allowance, turning in and stitching the opening closed as you sew.

7. Quilt the layers. I hand quilted 7 vertical lines of simple running stitches down the length of the quilt to secure the layers together, which I marked first using a hera marker. To mark these lines, use a long, clear quilter's ruler to loosely space out 7 lines across the quilt top. Position the ruler in place, and run the hera marker along its edge to make a visible crease line on the surface. Repeat for each line. Use a length of sashiko thread no longer than the length of your arm to create the running stitches, burying the knots between the layers. Use a thimble to protect the finger that will do the work of pushing the needle through the fabric.

8. Label your quilt following the instructions on page 156.

8

Value

Several years ago, my friend Katie Pedersen of the blog *Sew Katie Did* introduced me to the idea of playing with the color value of fabrics to create patterning in a quilt. I now find it one of my favorite ways to make sense of seemingly uncoordinated fabrics that have no relevance to each other. Vintage and collected fabrics that don't feel connected suddenly work together in a quilt using this method. Ignore the overall color palette for a moment, create stacks of prints based purely on their light and dark values, and suddenly you have cohesion where none was before.

The success of this quilt design rests on using as many fabrics as you can get your hands on. Sure, you could just go to the fabric store, but I encourage you to pull fabrics from your stash, especially the ones you maybe aren't so in love with. Take it a step further and use collecting fabrics as an excuse to spend time with those important people in your life who are happy to share their stories and swap fabrics. So many of us have more fabric than we will ever use. Present the idea of this quilt to friends and family and you will soon be overflowing with fabric scraps.

This quilt is not complicated, and once you master the half-square triangle technique required, you can do all the steps in batches, streamlining the process. I discovered so much joy in the design of this quilt; I hope you give it a try!

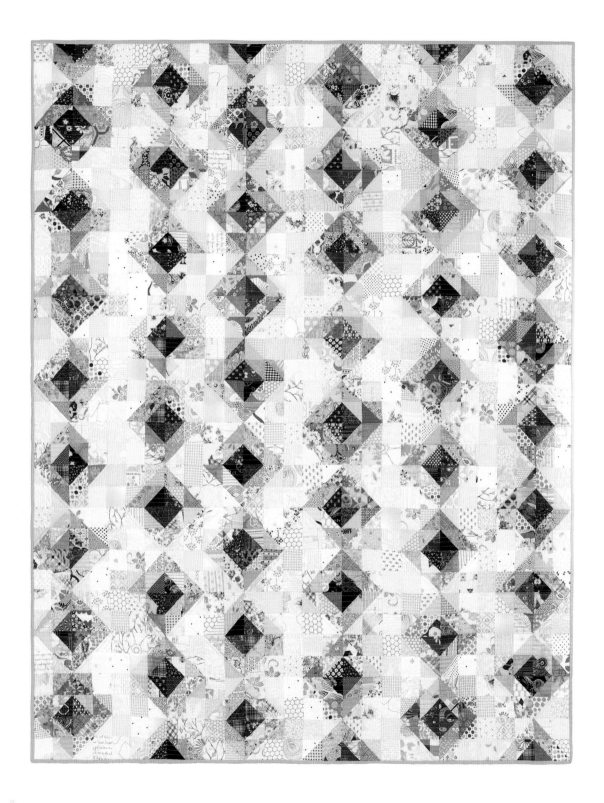

Finished Quilt Size:
56 × 68 inches,
for a throw-sized quilt

Finished Block Size:
2 × 2 inches

Techniques: Creating design
using color values, making half-
square triangles

Fabrics

For the Feature Fabric: Cotton weight quilting fabrics
in the following amounts: 1¼ yards total of dark-value
scraps; 3¼ yards total of medium-value scraps; and 3¼
yards total of light-value scraps.

For the Backing: 4¼ yards 44-inch-wide quilting cotton. Backing should be least 4 inches larger than your
quilt top's total length and width.

For the Binding: ½ yard 44-inch-wide quilting cotton
in a coordinating color

Feature Fabric Suggestions: Vintage fabric, feed
sacks, and other quilting weight cottons or cotton/poly
fabrics will work here. Save any heavier fabrics for
another project. Solid will work, but patterned fabrics
will create the liveliest design effect.

Other Materials

Low-Loft Cotton
Batting: 1 package
twin-sized batting
cut to size. Batting
should be least 4
inches larger than
your quilt top's total
length and width.

My Color and Design Notes

Sort every fabric you have into three piles according to
light, medium, and dark values. Do not overthink this
step; it works best if you just quickly sort them all. If
any just do not seem to fall anywhere, put those aside
during that first sort. They will naturally fit into one of
the value piles as the design grows.

You will most likely have an abundance of medium-
value fabrics, so keep in mind that these can read
darker or lighter based on where they are positioned in
the design. A subtle value shift is all you need to create
the pattern.

A fabric may feel like a light value in one block but may
work better as a medium value in another block. Be
open to these subtle changes; they can create a very
interesting design.

Remember to stop periodically and study this design
from afar. I actually made a mistake in mine—maybe
you can spot it? It's subtle, but it's there. My long arm
quilter thought it was intentional so went with it. It is so
fascinating how I can work so closely on a design and
never see something left out. I don't view it as a mistake
now that the quilt is done. It is more a part of this quilt's
story, adding a "spot the difference" element.

I used a solid pale green flannel from my collection for
the backing. Flannel is a cozy backing for any quilt, and
if you don't have enough fabric, consider repurposing a
flannel sheet.

PREPARE AND SORT THE FABRICS

1. Refer to the section Preparing Vintage and Secondhand Fabric on page 150 for information on preparing your fabric.

2. Sort all the fabrics into 3 stacks: dark, medium, and light value.

CUT THE FABRICS

3. Cut the fabric into squares measuring 3¼ inches as follows: 102 squares from the dark-value fabrics; 306 squares from the medium-value fabrics; 204 squares from the light-value fabrics. In addition, cut 340 squares measuring 2½ inches from the light-value fabrics.

MAKE THE HALF-SQUARE TRIANGLES

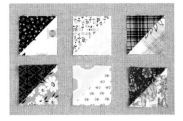

a.

4. Use only the 3¼-inch squares to make the half-square triangle units. To make a pair of half-square triangle units, pair 2 fabric squares, right sides together, making sure there is good contrast between the 2 fabrics. Pair 102 dark values to 102 medium values to create 204 half-square triangle units. Pair 204 medium values to 204 light values to create 408 half-square triangle units.

Once you have paired 2 fabric squares together, draw a diagonal line across the wrong side of the lighter square with a Frixion pen or pencil, diagonally from one top corner to the bottom opposite corner. At the sewing machine, stitch the pair together, ¼ inch away from the drawn line, on both sides of the line. (Tip: I like to chain piece these squares by feeding the pairs through the machine one after the other without cutting thread, sewing along one side of the line, then feeding the squares through to sew on the other side of the line.) Once all the pairs are sewn together, cut each pair in half on the drawn line. At the ironing board, press the seam allowances toward the darker fabric, and square up the resulting 2 half-square triangle units to measure 2½ × 2½ inches (see a).

LAY OUT THE DESIGN

5. On a design wall or cleared space, arrange the units to create the diamond-shape blocks (see b), following the illustration (see c). Distribute like colors throughout the design, and use a reducing glass to stand back from the design and ensure a clear pattern is emerging. Once the layout feels right, snap a picture of it to refer to later.

b.

CONSTRUCT THE QUILT TOP

6. Starting at the top and working in columns from left to right down the quilt, remove the first column of blocks from the design wall and sew them together. Repeat this step with each column, putting it back up on the design wall once sewn. Press each column's seam allowances to the opposing sides to nest the seams when the columns are sewn together.

7. Sew the quilt columns to each other, from the left to right across the quilt top. Several points will match up between each column, and I find that nesting the seams, holding them in place with a pin or sewing stiletto, and guiding them slowly under the presser foot helps them line up. Press the seam allowances to one consistent side.

c.

FINISH THE QUILT

Refer to Quilting 101 (page 145) for more information on each of these steps.

8. If needed, piece fabric together to make the quilt backing, which should measure at least 4 inches larger than the finished top's length and width. Layer the quilt backing, batting, and quilt top to create a quilt sandwich of all 3 layers. Pin baste the layers together.

9. Quilt the layers. This is the only quilt in the book that I had professionally quilted, and my quilter, Krista Withers of Krista Withers Quilting, did a beautiful job of helping further define the pattern I created. She did some simple outlining of the darker diamond shapes and a muted pattern of swirls throughout the lighter areas.

10. When the quilting is completed, trim the quilt layers to be 56 × 68 inches or your desired size.

11. Prepare the binding and bind the quilt following the instructions on page 154.

12. Label your quilt following the instructions on page 156.

9

D'Orly

Vintage handkerchiefs are beautiful and fun to collect. The brightly colored, floral ones with the scalloped edges are some of my favorites, and their colors are just as vivid today as they must have been back in their early days. These delicate pieces of fabric are reminiscent of the prim and proper ladies from my childhood. Probably more decorative accessories than functional items, these handkerchiefs may have been folded and pinned to a coat lapel, waved in the air to get someone's attention, or dabbed at a tear or two, but nothing more—and most likely never touched a runny nose. I used my collection of Jean D'Orly handkerchiefs to create this quilt. Their sketchy patterns and color combos feel quite modern and are some of my favorites. As with every collection I cut into to make a quilt, my apprehension at getting started forces me to begin by cutting into my least favorite ones first, but soon enough I get excited to cut into every one of them.

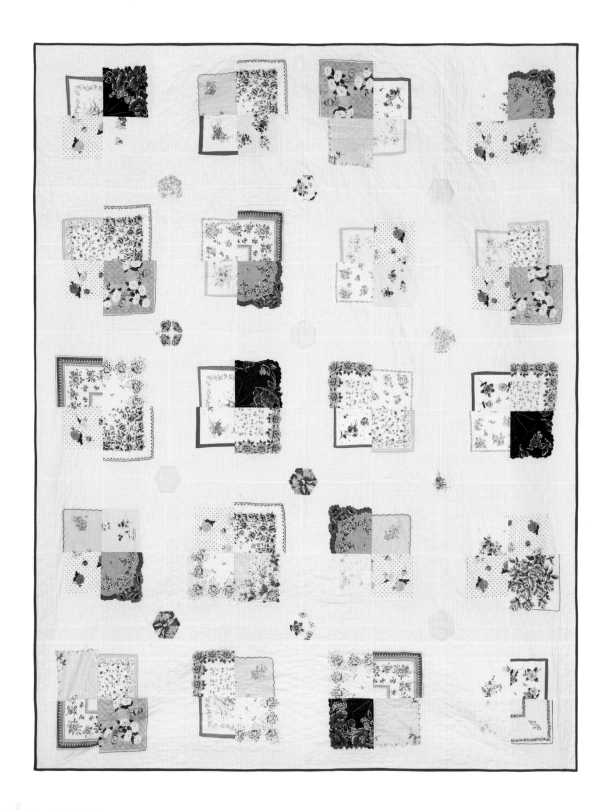

Finished Quilt Size:
76 × 95 inches,
for a full-sized quilt

Finished Block Size:
19 × 19 inches

Techniques: Reinforcing light woven fabrics to use in patchwork, free motion quilting using stencils, fussy cutting, English paper piecing

Fabrics

For the Feature Fabric: 24 cotton or linen handkerchiefs

For the Top: 5 yards 44-inch-wide quilting cotton in a solid color

For the Backing: 8½ yards quilting cotton. Backing should be least 4 inches larger than your quilt top's length and width.

For the Binding: ¾ yard of 44-inch-wide quilting cotton in a coordinating color

Feature Fabric Suggestion: The handkerchiefs I used ranged in size; the smallest was 10½ inches square, and the largest was 14½ inches square. Four of the handkerchiefs will be used to make paper-pieced hexagons. This quilt would also be fun with men's monogrammed hankies or bandanas.

Other Materials

Ultra lightweight fusible interfacing: 8 yards (I used Pellon #12005096.)

Low-Loft Cotton Batting: 1 package queen-sized batting cut to size; backing should be least 4 inches larger than your quilt top's length and width.

Flower quilting stencil (#ZNC-036-08, available from The Stencil Co)

English piecing 3-inch-size hexagon paper template (available online at PaperPieces.com)

My Color and Design Notes

I challenged myself to create a quilt top that was more than just a patchwork of the handkerchiefs. The solid background keeps this design from being too girly and breaks up the patterning of the handkerchiefs in an unexpected way.

Vintage handkerchiefs may at first glance look square, but in fact, they rarely are. The forgiving nature of this quilt design prevents their unevenness from being a problem.

If you are adding to an existing hankie collection or looking to start your own, I would encourage you to let the color palette happen naturally. I, myself, was unsure about some of the dark gray ones, yet they turned out to be just what my piece needed.

Variety in color and pattern will create a lively design and contrast well against the solid background. More daintily printed hankies can blend with the background and create a more muted design.

An embroidered "S" in one corner of an otherwise plain hankie that wasn't part of my original design was cut and added in at one of the corners, right at the last minute. Never be so tightly tied to a theme or fabric story that you are not open to fun little details like this.

PREPARE THE FABRICS

1. Refer to the section Preparing Vintage and Secondhand Fabric on page 150 for information on preparing your fabric. The dye on hankies such as these is generally very colorfast, but consider using a color catcher in the wash load to absorb any dye in the wash water if that is a concern. Dry and press, using a flattening spray for the handkerchiefs to remove wrinkles.

2. Add stabilizer to the handkerchiefs. Following the manufacturer's instructions, add the fusible interfacing to the back of the handkerchiefs to stabilize them. Cut a piece roughly the size of the hankie (maybe slightly smaller so you won't fuse it to your ironing board), and place it on the back of the hankie. Cover the squares with a press cloth and iron them to fuse the interfacing to the back of each handkerchief (see a). Repeat to stabilize all the handkerchiefs. Set aside the 4 handkerchiefs that will be used for the hand-appliquéd hexagons for now.

a.

CUT AND SEW THE FABRIC

3. Cut twenty 20-inch squares from the background fabric.

4. To find the exact center of each background square, fold it into quarters. Lightly press the square with an iron to mark the crease. Do the same with each of the handkerchiefs.

b.

5. Place a handkerchief on a background square, both with right sides facing up and lining up the creases to center the hankie on the square. Pin to secure. Machine stitch the hankie on the background square along its edge; use a neutral thread that blends to do this—no need to get crazy trying to match thread to every hankie (see b). Repeat this step for all 20 squares.

6. Cut each of these squares into 4 equal pieces measuring 10 × 10 inches.

LAY OUT THE DESIGN

7. On a design wall or cleared space, arrange the pieces, following the illustration (see c) for general placement. The goal is to create new, mismatched blocks with 4 different handkerchiefs, using the photo for reference. Spread the darker patterns evenly around the quilt. Once the layout feels right, snap a picture of it to refer to later. (Tip: I sewed each of the blocks together as noted in the next step and repositioned them on the wall to be sure that I was happy with placement before proceeding.)

c.

CONSTRUCT THE QUILT TOP

8. I constructed my quilt in 4 patch blocks, then sewed the blocks to each other in rows from the top to the bottom of the quilt top. To do this, take the 4 pieces that make up 1 block down from the design wall. Sew the top 2 pieces together, and press the seam allowance to the one side. Next sew the bottom pieces

together, pressing the seam allowance in the opposite direction. Sew the 2 top and bottom pieces of the block together and press the seam allowance to one side. Check that the block is 19½ × 19½ inches and trim to square up if necessary. Put the completed block back on the wall, and repeat this step with the next block. You will have a total of 20 blocks measuring 19½ × 19½ inches.

9. Sew the blocks to each other in rows going across the quilt first, pressing the seam allowances for each row in opposite directions so the seams will nest and line up when sewing the rows to each other.

10. Last, sew the rows to each other, from the top to the bottom of the quilt top. Press the seam allowances to the same side.

FINISH THE QUILT

Refer to Quilting 101 (page 145) for more information on each of these steps.

11. If needed, piece fabric together to make the quilt backing, which should measure at least 4 inches larger than the finished top's length and width. Layer the quilt backing, batting, and quilt top to create a quilt sandwich of all 3 layers. Pin baste the layers together.

12. Quilt the layers. I was very inspired by the motifs on the handkerchiefs and did a free motion loop-d-loop design in white thread around each of the handkerchiefs on the background squares, roughly marking the design first with a Frixion or water-soluble marking pen. From there, I wanted to quilt something inside the handkerchief area of each block, but because they are all so different, I settled on 1 flower stencil motif to put in the center of all of them, which helped to add some unity to the overall design. I centered the stencil and marked it directly on the block centers, then stitched it with free motion quilting (see c).

13. Create and add the paper-pieced hexagons to the quilt top. I used a total of 12 paper-pieced hexagon shapes created from the 4 handkerchiefs that were set aside in step 2. These are hand sewn onto the quilt between each of the squares (see c). To create the hexagon pieces, the fabric must first be basted to the paper template. I used a water-soluble glue pen to glue baste these. To do this, roughly cut an area from one of the handkerchiefs ¼ inch larger than the paper piece. (Note: No need for exact cutting. Just allow enough fabric to wrap around to the back of the paper.) If desired, you can "fussy cut" a specific area of the design you want to center in the hexagon. Place the paper piece on the wrong side of the fabric in the center. Working on the back of the paper template, apply glue along 1 edge of the side of the paper template. Wrap that edge of the fabric to the back of the paper, allowing the glue to hold it down. Repeat on all edges of the paper template, folding all the corner edges neatly toward the back and securing down. At the ironing board, use a dry iron to press from the front of each hexagon to crease the edges well. Carefully remove the paper from the fabric, press again on both sides, and the hexagon shape should be set and ready to sew on the quilt top. Do this to create 12 hexagons.

14. Hand stitch each hexagon centered in the seam area (see c). These are sewn onto the quilt top, not through all the quilt layers. Pin in position, then sew them in place with small slip stitches.

15. When the quilting and hand sewing are complete, trim the edges of all the quilt layers to be even on all 4 sides, measuring 76 × 95 inches or your desired size.

16. Prepare the binding and bind the quilt following the instructions on page 154.

17. Label your quilt following the instructions on page 156.

10

Frock

The wedding dress is one of the most life-changing garments a woman will ever wear, and for that reason, I knew I wanted to make a quilt with one. My friend Melissa offered her own wedding dress, worn fifteen years ago when she wed her husband, Paul.

The idea of a wedding dress quilt was one thing, but actually cutting into a dress of a dear friend was another thing altogether. I was nervous. I put it off for months. Until one day, when I knew I had to tackle this project head-on. As I started planning and sketching, it occurred to me that her dress had been wrapped in tissue in my studio for a long time. Most likely it had been stowed away similarly at her house. Who was enjoying this dress all wrapped up and stored away? Having this dress out on my worktable made me think daily about what special people Melissa and Paul are and how their lives are such an inspiration to me. Having the dress out of storage brought so much positivity to me every time I looked at it.

I am now firmly in the camp of making something special out of a special dress you will probably only wear once. I called this quilt project *Frock* because any special-occasion dress could be celebrated this way. Creating this wall hanging from Melissa's dress has revived its spirit and illuminated its symbolism in a completely new and unexpected way. I used the classic Courthouse Steps patchwork pattern to create the blocks for this wall hanging.

Working with fabrics such as silks, satins, crepe de chines—all the fine fabrics a special-occasion dress could be made of—can be tricky. They slip, are fussy to press, and the edges can fray. There are some considerations that make working with these fabrics much easier to manage.

Melissa had told me that she would have chosen a different color for her bridesmaid's dresses. Thinking about this, I decided to create an assortment of color options in the center of each block out of vintage satin and silk coat linings. I will show you how to piece these small pieces together onto a muslin foundation for a sturdy, well-constructed block.

Finished Quilt Size: 24 × 36 inches, for a wall hanging

Finished Block Size: 12 × 12 inches

Techniques: Using unconventional fabric for patchwork, improvisational piecing, foundation piecing, adding embellishments to the quilt surface, free motion quilting, adding a quilt sleeve.

Fabrics

For the Feature Fabric: Wedding dress; assorted scraps of special fabrics for the block centers (I used 15 different colors.)

For Piecing: ¼ yard cotton muslin

For the Backing: 1½ yards 44-inch-wide quilting cotton. Backing should be least 4 inches larger than your quilt top's total length and width.

For the Binding: ¼ yard 44-inch-wide quilting cotton in a coordinating color or enough extra fabric from the dress for the binding (I used fabric from the dress.)

Feature Fabric Suggestion: It's helpful if the wedding dress has a minimum of 2 fabrics to work with. Consider the lining of the dress as a fabric option, as well as the back of the fabrics. These can add a subtle contrast to the dress fabric. For the block centers, choose high contrast colors that will stand out against the main dress fabric that will surround them. I used a variety of satins, silks, and polyester dress linings. Avoid thick fabrics, but this is a good place to use small bits of fabric you love. Save any details from the dress, such as buttons or beads, to use as surface embellishments.

Other Materials

Low Loft Cotton Batting: 28 × 41 inches. Batting should be least 4 inches larger than your quilt top's total length and width.

Sew-on Swarovski Crystals: I used "pure leaf" and "round chessboard" sew-on crystals in assorted colors (available online at www.fusionbeads.com).

26-inch-wide wooden dowel, cut to size, for hanging

My Color and Design Notes

I wanted to have some subtle pattern shifts in the cream fabric strips surrounding the colored centers, but this is not necessary. To achieve this effect, I used the lace overlay bodice fabric from Melissa's dress, as well as the skirt and lining fabric. But I needed a fourth cream fabric, so I made a trip to the fabric store and found a cream crepe that blended well with the other three fabrics. This addition allowed me to create the symmetrical design I had in my mind's eye.

You may need to open up the seams of the dress to get to the fabric you'd like to use. Unpick seams from the wrong side of the dress whenever you can.

Consider all the details from the day that could be added: pearls, sparkles, tablecloth and napkin prints, silk flowers, ribbons, hair adornments, buttons, anything significant that could be sewn on. As a wall hanging, these surface embellishments will add another layer of interest and beauty.

I intentionally constructed the block centers before cutting into the wedding dress. It is just plain scary to take scissors to a wedding dress! When it's time, remember the first cut is the hardest, and make it easier by cutting into the hem. This will help you gain your courage.

Each of the blocks is sewn a bit oversized to compensate for finicky fabrics and how they can be tricky to sew. You will square up and, if necessary, trim each block once they are completed.

PREPARE THE DRESS AND OTHER FABRICS

1. Refer to the section Preparing Vintage and Secondhand Fabric on page 150 for information on preparing your fabric. For Melissa's dress, I cut away all the buttons from the back of the bodice (those became the center of the flowers I sewed on later). Next I used a seam ripper to gently coax the side seams of the bodice apart. You don't need to undo every single seam, especially in the smaller pieces. Instead, when cutting your strips, just act like they are not there and make straight cuts. A seam included in the strip will just add character.

CREATE THE PIECED CENTER SQUARES

a.

2. Cut six 5½-inch squares from the muslin. The small scraps that make up the center block will be sewn to the muslin, a technique known as foundation piecing. This will help to add stability and structure to all those little pieces. Place the first scrap, right side up, anywhere on top of the muslin. Lay the next piece directly over the first, right sides together, lining up their edges. Sew the pieces together along the edge using a ¼-inch seam allowance (see a). Fold the scraps open and press them flat, using a press cloth, if needed. Add the next scrap over what you've just sewn, finding another straight edge to line it up to, right sides together. Sew, press seam open, and repeat. This method allows oddly shaped pieces to fit together smoothly, without puckering. Continue adding pieces of fabric until you have covered the entire muslin square.

3. When you've covered the muslin square, trim the entire block down to be 4½ inches square (see b).

You will need 6 blocks.

b.

CONSTRUCT THE BLOCKS

4. Using a long quilter's ruler at least 2 inches wide, cut 2-inch-wide strips from the wedding dress fabric (see outline on the opposite page). Each Courthouse Step block was constructed of 2 different cream fabrics surrounding the center square. Because I had 4 different fabrics, in my version I made 3 blocks using 2 of the fabrics and 3 blocks using the other 2 fabrics. Each block needs the following strips:

FABRIC A

Two strips 2 × 4½ inches

Two strips 2 × 7½ inches

Two strips 2 × 10¾ inches

FABRIC B

Two strips 2 × 7½ inches

Two strips 2 × 10¾ inches

Two strips 2 × 13¾ inches

You will make 6 blocks.

5. To make 1 block, lay out one of the pieced center squares. Place a strip of Fabric A, 2 × 4½ inches, to the top and bottom of the square, right sides together. Pin it in place, stitch, and press open, always pressing the seam allowances toward the newest piece sewn on (see c). (Tip: I found a sewing stiletto helped to keep the slippery, layered fabrics in place as they went under the presser foot.)

6. Next, sew a strip of Fabric B, 2 × 7½ inches, to the opposite sides of the center square, right sides together. Pin the pieces in place, stitch, and press. Sew a strip of Fabric A, 2 × 7½ inches, to the top and bottom of the block. Sew a strip of Fabric B, 2 × 10¾ inches, to the opposite sides of the square.

For the last round, sew a strip of Fabric A, 2 × 10¾ inches, to the top and bottom of the block. Last, sew a strip of Fabric B, 2 × 13¾ inches, to the sides of the block.

7. Check that the final block is 12½ inches square, trimming to square it up only if necessary. Repeat steps 5 through 7 for all 6 blocks.

LAY OUT THE QUILT TOP

8. Place the blocks on a design wall or cleared surface and play with how the fabrics are positioned from one block to the next (see d). You should have 3 rows of 2 blocks each. Once you have a layout that works, take a picture of it to refer to before moving on.

CONSTRUCT THE QUILT TOP

9. Sew the quilt together first in rows from left to right. Press the seam allowances of each row to the opposite side so the seams will nest when the rows

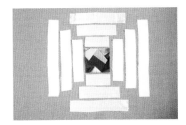

c.

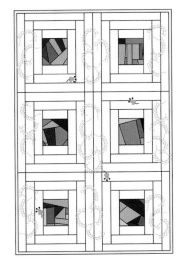

d.

are sewn together. Next sew the rows together from top to bottom. Press the seam allowances to one side or the other. Just stay consistent. The quilt top is done.

FINISH THE QUILT

Refer to Quilting 101 (page 145) for more information on each of these steps.

10. Make your quilt backing, then layer the quilt back, batting, and quilt top to create a quilt sandwich of all 3 layers. Pin baste the layers together.

11. Quilt the layers using free motion embroidery. I was inspired by the lace fabric to stitch simple vine-like shapes, which I first practiced drawing on paper. I used matching thread and stitched vines and leaves across the surface, but only a few. I wanted the bridal fabric to be the feature. I also carefully stitched in the ditch around the center square blocks (see d).

12. Embellish the quilt top. I used the buttons from Melissa's dress to make flowers at the tips of the stitched vines and stitched them through the quilt top and batting only; I buried my beginning and ending thread tails in the batting. I also added sew-on Swarovski crystals in colors pulled from the center squares, just to add some additional sparkle. I wanted to give the piece movement as one walked by it, and these will reflect light beautifully. Add embellishments, taking time to step back and view your entire piece from a distance to see what's working.

13. When the quilting is complete and the embellishments sewn on, trim the edges of all the quilt layers to be even on all 4 sides, measuring 24 × 36 inches or your desired size.

14. Prepare the binding and bind the quilt following the instructions on page 154.

15. Label your quilt following the instructions on page 156.

16. Make a hanging sleeve following the instructions on page 157.

11

Spirit

There is a tradition in the history of quilt making referred to as the "humility block." Historians describe it as an imperfect patchwork block or odd piece of fabric sewn intentionally into a quilt by the maker. This was done to create an imperfect quilt, because only God is perfect, and the idea of making a perfect quilt would be considered prideful and conceited. I have always loved the idea of the humility block. Quilts require time, intention, and care from their makers, and seeing the hand that sewed them in the work only adds to their beauty, their physical and metaphorical warmth. (I, myself, will never be faced with needing to *intentionally* add mistakes into my quilts.)

The quilt projects in this book are all well and good if you have a quantity of textiles to choose from. But what about that one special fabric, the one you may only have a scrap of? Maybe it's the few inches left of a favorite childhood doll's dress or remnants of a much loved tattered blanket. I created this quilt with those coveted pieces of fabric in mind. You choose, treasure hunt, or simply buy new all the main fabrics in the quilt. The "spirit cloth," or humility scrap, will be sewn in to only one spot of your choosing, becoming a memorable focus of the entire piece.

For my own quilt, I used a blue-green wool plaid that exemplifies my journey as a maker. I found the original skirt it came from in a thrift store many years ago. Over the years of blogging at *Wise Craft Handmade*, I have cut fabric from that skirt to make everything from soft toys for my kids to handbags, pillows, and quilts. This fabric has worked hard for me, and I love how it feels celebrated in this quilt.

This quilt is constructed in blocks, with strips of fabric added between each of the blocks, called "sashing." To create the trees, you will need either a specialty Tri-Recs ruler set or the templates included in the back of the book.

Finished Quilt Size: 56 × 68 inches, for a throw-sized quilt

Finished Block Size: 8 × 12 inches

Techniques: Using templates or specialty rulers, piecing angles, incorporating sashing strips between blocks and rows, hand quilting, free motion quilting

Fabrics

For the Feature Fabric: A piece or scrap of special fabric for one spirit block measuring at least 7 × 7 inches

For the Top: 4 yards 44-inch-wide quilting cotton in a solid color for the background; six men's cotton dress shirts or 5 or 6 different colors totaling ¼ yard 44-inch-wide quilting cotton for the trees (I used 6 different men's cotton shirts from the thrift store); several colors of small brown scrap fabrics for the trunks

For the Backing: 4¼ yards 44-inch-wide quilting cotton. Backing should be least 4 inches larger than your quilt top's total length and width.

For the Binding: ½ yard 44-inch-wide quilting cotton in a coordinating color

Feature Fabric Suggestions: Most any fabric will work as long as it isn't too thick. Fabrics like cotton similar to a quilting or home décor weight, lightweight wool, corduroy, silk are ideal. Even a light leather could work with a little extra care.

Other Materials

Wool Batting: 1 package twin-sized batting cut to size. Batting should be least 4 inches larger than your quilt top's length and width. (I used Hobb's lightweight, washable wool batting.)

A Tri-Recs ruler set or the templates on page 160 (I used Wrights EZ Tri-Recs Quilt Ruler set.)

Template plastic available at quilting and craft stores (optional, if using templates)

My Color and Design Notes

This quilt was created and sewn in autumn, and I am sure that influenced my color palette and design. I had the red, mustard, and tan men's shirts from previous thrift store trips, and I loved the way they allowed the plaid cloth to stand out and be noticed. I chose not to have the spirit cloth blend at all. This was a design choice, and you may want the colors of your quilt to work together entirely differently. Think about how much contrast you want between the major fabrics and the spirit cloth in your quilt and stick to that palette range.

I'm usually a fan of doing all the cutting and piecing in batches for efficiency, but I wanted to see how much of each color I wanted in the design as I went along, so I cut and pieced only a few blocks at a time. If a color seemed to work well, I would make more of that block before moving forward. Sometimes it makes more sense to consider the design in bits, rather than deciding the full palette at the beginning. Be open to color and pattern surprises as you create the individual blocks.

For my quilt, only the large back panels of each of the shirts I used were needed. I saved the rest of the shirts for another project.

This quilt makes efficient use of the background yardage that goes around each of the trees. Each tree block will take up one entire strip cut selvedge to selvedge, with just a bit left over.

The loft and thickness of the wool batting I chose allowed for a cuddly, light as air, breathable warmth.

If you use the templates included, print them out at full size. Cut them out, glue them onto a piece of template plastic, cut out the plastic and place them on the fabric, and trace around them. This rigid form will prevent the template from losing its shape.

I chose to use the background fabric as my binding for a subtle effect.

PREPARE THE FABRICS

1. Refer to the section Preparing Vintage and Secondhand Fabric on page 150 for information on preparing your fabric.

CUT THE FABRICS

2. From the shirts, cut 2½-inch-wide strips across the longest part of the shirt panel. The length of these strips will vary for each shirt, but for now, assume 1 cut strip will create all the pieces needed for 1 tree block and cut the number of strips needed for all the blocks in that color. Or, do as I did: cut a few strips, create a few blocks, and decide if that color works in the design before cutting more.

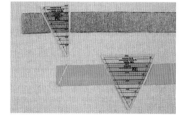

a.

3. Sub cut the shirt strips, cutting through 1 layer of fabric at a time, using either a Tri tool, or the tree template as follows: Align the 6½-inch line of the Tri tool (Line A) with the bottom edge of the strip. Cut out this shape. Rotate the Tri tool or template 180 degrees (do not turn it over), align the 5½-inch line (Line B) with the top edge of the fabric strip, and cut. Rotate the Tri tool 180 degrees again and align the 4½-inch line (Line C) with the bottom edge, and cut. Rotate 180 degrees and align the 3½-inch line (Line D) with the top edge, and cut. Rotate 180 degrees and align the 2½-inch line (Line E) with the bottom edge of the fabric strip and cut (see a). Last, rotate the Tri tool 180 degrees and align the 1½-inch line (Line F) with the top edge of the fabric, and cut. Repeat this step for each block for a total of 35 blocks.

4. From the background fabric, measure and cut 48 strips measuring 2½ × 44 inches (cut from selvedge to selvedge). Set aside 7 of these strips to use for the binding.

5. Fold each background strip in half lengthwise before cutting. This fold will allow you to cut through 2 layers at a time and create mirror images of each piece, which is necessary to make the pieces sewn to both sides of the tree strips. Begin by cutting away the selvedges and squaring up the edge of the strip. Measure and cut 3 inches from the squared off edges; these will be sewn to both sides of the tree trunk.

6. Sub cut the remainder of each strip using either a Recs ruler tool or the background template as follows: Align the 6½-inch line (Line G) of the ruler with the bottom edge of the fabric strip, and cut. Rotate the ruler 180 degrees, align the 5½-inch line (Line H) with the top edge of the fabric strip, and cut. Rotate and position to cut at the 4½-inch line (Line I). Rotate and position to cut at the 3½-inch line (Line J). Rotate and position to cut at the 2½-inch line (Line K), and last, rotate and position to cut at the 1½-inch line (Line L), and cut. Square off the edge of what remains of the strip; it will be sewn on to the finished blocks as a sashing strip (see c). Repeat for each block for a total of 35 blocks.

7. Cut 1 tree trunk from a brown fabric scrap measuring 2½ × 1½ inches. Repeat for a total of 35 trunks.

CONSTRUCT THE BLOCKS

Note: I constructed these blocks one at a time, in order not to get confused, and I recommend laying out the pieces for the block in the correct order before sewing it together, as the pieces look similar (see b). Sewing triangles and angled sides together can be tricky. Offset the top and bottom edges of the angled pieces by ¼ inch when sewing them together, so that the pieces will line up when turned and pressed (see more about sewing triangles in step 8 of *Taupe*, page 85).

8. Start sewing from the bottom of the block and move upward. Sew a 3-inch rectangle of background fabric to both sides of the trunk piece, right sides together. Press seam allowances toward the trunk.

9. Sew the 2½-inch Recs/K background pieces to either side of the 5½-inch Tri/B tree piece. Sew the 3½-inch Recs/J background pieces to both sides of the 4½-inch Tri/C tree piece. Sew the 4½-inch Recs/I background pieces to both sides of the 3½-inch Tri/D tree pieces. Sew the 5½-inch Recs/H background pieces to both sides of the 2½-inch Tri/E tree piece. Press all seam allowances toward the background fabric.

10. The top of the tree block is sewn a little differently than the others. To sew the 1½-inch Tri/F pieces to the 6½-inch Recs/G background piece, begin by sewing the right side of the 6½-inch Recs/G piece on to the Tri/F piece first,

b.

pressing the seam allowance to the background fabric. Next, repeat for the left side, press. Note that the two 6½-inch Recs/G background pieces should overlap at the top of the triangle by ¼ inch. This will ensure the top point of the triangle isn't cut off when the block is constructed. (Note: These units will have what is referred to as "dog ears" at the center top of the block. Snip these away to reduce overall bulk.)

11. To finish constructing the tree block, sew the units together from top to bottom. Press all seam allowances toward the trunk.

12. Sew the long background strip (set aside in step 6) to the right vertical side of the tree block, pressing the seam allowance toward the strip (see c). Square up and, if necessary, trim the entire block to measure 8½ × 12½ inches. Note: You will only add the sashing strip to 33 of the 35 blocks. For 2 of the blocks, leave this sashing strip off.

c.

13. Choose 2 blocks with sashing strips on the right and sew another sashing strip to the left side. These blocks will be used on the left edge of the second and fourth rows to offset the rows from the others. You should have a total of 2 blocks with no sashing strips added, 2 blocks with sashing strips added to both sides, and 31 blocks with sashing strips added only to the right side.

14. Piece the long sashing strips between rows. Each row is separated by a sashing strip of background fabric, which was cut and set aside in step 4. For my quilt, I wanted the seam line where I joined these strips together to land in a different spot on every row, so I pieced all 7 strips of ground fabric end to end to create one long strip, which I then sub cut into 56½-inch-long strips. You will need a total of 4 sashing strips measuring 2½ × 56½ inches.

LAY OUT THE DESIGN

15. On a design wall or cleared space, arrange the 35 blocks, following the illustration (see d), in 5 rows of 7 blocks each. Distribute colors throughout the design, so the eye will travel around all areas of the quilt top. Remember to offset the left side of the second and fourth rows as described in step 13 and shown in the illustration. Place 1 long sashing strip between each row as shown. Once the layout feels right, snap a picture of it to refer to later.

d.

CONSTRUCT THE QUILT TOP

16. Sew the quilt top together in rows, starting from the top left and going across. Sew the tree rows together, starting from the top. Sew 1 long sashing strip to the bottom of the top tree row, add the next tree row, add a sashing strip, and so on. Press all the seam allowances toward the sashing strips.

FINISH THE QUILT

Refer to Quilting 101 (page 145) for more information on each of these steps.

17. As needed, piece fabric together to make the quilt backing, which should measure at least 4 inches larger than the finished top's length and width. Layer the quilt backing, batting, and quilt top to create a quilt sandwich of all 3 layers. Pin baste the layers together.

18. Quilt the layers together. I wanted this quilt to feel billowy and lofty, not heavily quilted. I settled on a combination of hand quilting and free motion quilting to achieve that. First, I stitched a free motion loop-d-loop design on all of the background sashing strips with a coordinating thread (see d). If you would like to try this, draw a few out on paper for practice, then draw a few out directly on the quilt top with a fabric marking pen to guide you as you stitch. Doing free motion quilting beforehand allows you to remove the basting pins before settling into hand stitching and avoid getting poked.

19. I then hand quilted around each tree using several coordinating colors of size 8 Perle cotton thread and large quilting stitch. (Note: To avoid stitching through the seam allowance layers underneath, stitch a generous ¼ inch away from the seams.)

20. When the quilting is complete, trim the edges of all the quilt layers to be even on all 4 sides, measuring 56 × 68 inches or your desired size.

21. Prepare the binding and bind the quilt following the instructions on page 154.

22. Label your quilt following the instructions on page 156.

12

Star

There may be loved ones in your life that have a favorite "uniform." Be it an apron, a paint-stained artist's smock, or medical scrubs, one look at a particular garment and you just know to whom it belongs. In the form of shirts, it may be a favorite collection of flannel shirts or the Pinpoint oxfords our favorite men wear to the office. These pieces of clothing can evoke strong memories, and what better way to extend the life of garments past their prime and honor the person that wore them than sewing them into something beautiful and functional?

This star quilt is made of a collection of men's dress shirts, and the fabrics are finely woven dobby weaves and yarn dyed checks in a watery palette of blues, grays, and creams. The colors and tiny checks of my chosen collection reminded me of my husband Peter's daily work uniform, and the color palette felt cheerful and bright—perfect for a child's room. Pinpoint oxford shirting fabrics are more finely woven than quilting cottons. They are beautiful fabrics to quilt and usually have the patterning woven into the fabric, sometimes with a textural dobby weave. I love sewing with them.

This quilt is made of two basic blocks, and the large center sections in each are engineered to be large enough to include a full chest pocket. Having pockets for things like notes and stuffed animals is a delightful way to add character to a quilt's surface. I played with tonal value in this design, placing the light, medium, and dark values in specific positions in each block, but after a while I varied from that, as I usually do, and started mixing colors around a bit.

Finished Quilt Size:
65 × 78 inches,
for a throw- or twin-sized quilt

Finished Block Size:
13 × 13 inches

Techniques: Creating a design using color value, making Flying Geese units, adding unconventional details like pockets, free motion quilting

Fabrics

For the Feature Fabric: A variety of dress shirts in adult sizes

For the Backing: 6¼ yards 44-inch-wide quilting cotton. Backing should be at least 4 inches larger than your quilt top's total length and width.

For the Binding: ½ yard 44-inch-wide quilting cotton in a coordinating color

Feature Fabric Suggestion: I had a collection of 15 men's woven dress shirts in a variety of solids, stripes, checks, and jacquard weaves. Give yourself plenty of color and pattern options. Plaid, flannels, uniform shirts, and woven pajamas are all good options for this design.

Other Materials

Low-Loft Cotton Batting: Package of twin-sized batting cut to size. Backing should be least 4 inches larger than your quilt top's length and width.

My Color and Design Notes

I incorporated some shirt sleeves sent to me by my friend Erin, creator of the blog *House on Hill Road.* (Another way to get more patterns and weaves to choose from—share with friends!) I also made a trip to the thrift store to look for a couple of additional patterns and colors to help bring the whole design together. Supplement your assortment of shirts with interesting colors and patterns to complement your original collection and create a cohesive design.

The design will show best with a variety of light, medium, and dark values, but this can be interpreted loosely. For example, I randomly added in just a touch of a bright yellow check pattern, not paying attention to its value in relation to the other colors. A little of it does not overpower but adds movement. Unpredictability and surprise are aspects of quilt design that are fun to play with.

If you incorporate chest pockets or other details, as I did, a clear quilting ruler laid over that area can help you "fussy cut" out the part you want, allowing you to see through the ruler to be sure everything important is included. Always keep in mind the piece will lose ¼-inch seam allowance on each side, so be sure to take that into account as you position your ruler to cut.

I made myself a simple rule that the star blocks were the ones that would have the shirt pocket centers, but you could mix it up.

The free motion quilting I did around the star blocks is such a pretty effect, but it definitely took some time to complete. Sometimes a simple all-over stitch design can unify a quilt top. Other times, the quilting can add another element of visual interest to specific areas of the design. You choose what works best in your own design. I think this design would also be fun with simple, contrasting yarn ties.

If you are gifting this quilt to a child, consider putting a small present in one of the pockets, like a stuffed toy, to call attention to this added detail.

PREPARE THE FABRICS

1. Refer to the section Preparing Vintage and Secondhand Fabric on page 150 for information on preparing your fabric. If the shirts have been professionally laundered, consider washing and drying them to remove sizing.

CUT AND SORT THE SHIRTS

2. Cut the shirts to create the fabric for the quilt. I always cut close to the seams in this order: Cut away the collar, front placket, and sleeve cuffs. Cut close to the shirt's side seam, starting at the bottom hem, cutting all the way up the side, and continuing up the sleeve seam. Remove the side seam completely by cutting on both sides of it. Cut the sleeves away from the shirt body at the shoulder seams. Cut away the back yoke; if it is wide, try cutting it open at the seam to reveal an extra layer of useable fabric. Cut out and keep any interesting labels (those are fun to sew on to the quilt top).

3. Sort the fabric into 3 stacks: light, medium, and dark values. (Note: If one seems to fall into more than one value, just add it to the value stack that has the least amount of fabric.)

4. Cut the shirt fabric into squares as follows: From the light-value stack, cut one hundred twenty 3¾-inch squares (each block uses 4 of these squares, so be sure to cut sets of 4 from each shirt you use). From the medium-value stack, cut one hundred twenty 7 × 3¾-inch rectangles (again, each block uses 4, so cut in groups of 4). From the dark-value stack, cut thirty 7-inch squares. (If you are incorporating pockets from the dark fabric, use a large square ruler or draw a template in order to position the pocket in the center of the square you cut.) Also cut eight 3¾-inch squares to match each 7-inch square, for a total of 120.

CONSTRUCT THE BLOCKS

Note: I constructed the blocks for this quilt one at a time, to keep things in order and to allow me to tweak the design as I created the quilt top.

5. Construct the square blocks. Following the layout in the photo (see a), lay out each block in order by the sewing machine before sewing it together.

a.

ROW ONE

One light-value 3¾-inch square

One 3¾ × 7-inch medium-value rectangle

One light-value 3¾-inch square

One 3¾ × 7-inch medium-value rectangle

One dark-value 7-inch square

One 3¾ × 7-inch medium-value rectangle

ROW THREE

One light-value 3¾-inch square

One 3¾ × 7-inch medium-valued rectangle

One light-value 3¾-inch square

Sew the pieces together in rows from left to right and then sew the rows together top to bottom. Always press the seam allowances toward the medium-value pieces (this will allow the seams to "nest" together when sewing the rows to each other, which helps create perfect points). Press the finished block. Square up and, if necessary, trim each block to measure 13½ inches square. You will need 15 of these blocks.

6. Construct the star blocks. Begin by making the four Flying Geese units needed for the block. (Tip: A photo reference of how a basic Flying Geese unit is sewn can be found in *Leaving the Nest*, page 93.) Lay out 8 identical 3¾-inch dark-value squares on your worktable, wrong side up. Use a marking pen and a ruler to draw a diagonal line across the wrong side of each square, from top left to bottom right. This will be your stitching line. Next, lay 4 identical 3¾ × 7-inch medium-value rectangles on your work surface, right side up. Place 1 dark square over the right side of each rectangle, right sides together, right edges aligned, with the drawn line pointing up toward the top middle of the rectangle. At the sewing machine, stitch on the drawn line. Trim away excess fabric on the side of the stitch line closest to the corner, leaving a ¼-inch seam allowance. Press the unit open, pressing seam allowances toward the newly added square.

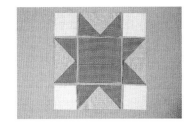

b.

Repeat this step on the left side, placing the drawn sewing line going up toward the top middle of the rectangle (it should overlap the previous seam by about ¼ inch). Stitch on the line, trim away excess fabric on the side of the stitch line closest to the corner, leaving a ¼-inch seam allowance. Press the unit open, pressing seam allowances toward the newly added square. Check that your finished Flying Geese unit measures 3¾ × 7 inches; trim if necessary. You will need 4 identical Flying Geese units for each of the 15 star blocks, for a total of 60 units.

Lay out the entire star block in order near your sewing machine, as noted on the next page, from left to right (see b).

ROW ONE

One light-value 3¾-inch square

One Flying Geese unit placed with point toward center of the block

One light-value 3¾-inch square

ROW TWO

One Flying Geese unit placed with point toward center of the block

One dark-value 7-inch square

One Flying Geese unit placed with point facing toward center of the block

ROW THREE

One light-value 3¾-inch square

One Flying Geese unit placed with point facing center of the block

One light-value 3¾-inch square

Sew the block together, first in rows from left to right. Always press the seam allowances away from the Flying Geese unit, and the seams and points will nest nicely.

Sew the rows to each other from top to bottom. Press the seam allowances going in the same direction. Square up and, if necessary, trim each block to measure 13½ inches square. You will need 15 of these blocks.

LAY OUT THE DESIGN

7. On a design wall, lay out the design following the illustration (see c), alternating the star and square blocks, to create 6 rows of 5 blocks each. Play with placement of colors and blocks until you are happy with the design. It is helpful to use a reducing glass to stand back and take in the entire design and see how the value differences look. When you are pleased with the layout, snap a photo to refer to during construction of the quilt.

CONSTRUCT THE QUILT TOP

8. Sew the quilt top together in rows, starting from the top left and going across, pressing each row's seam allowances in the opposite direction from the previous one so they will nest together nicely when joined.

9. Next, sew the rows together, starting from the top. Press the seam allowances in the same direction.

c.

FINISH THE QUILT

Refer to Quilting 101 (page 145) for more information on each of these steps.

10. As needed, piece fabric together to make the quilt backing, which should measure at least 4 inches larger than the finished top's length and width. Layer the quilt backing, batting, and quilt top to create a quilt sandwich of all 3 layers. Pin baste the layers together.

11. Quilt the layers. I chose to do all free motion quilting on this quilt. I loved the subtlety of the overall palette, but I wanted to place a little more emphasis on the blocks with the stars (those are the ones in which I included the shirt pockets). I used a coordinating light blue thread and my free motion foot to stitch swirly shapes surrounding the stars, and I also stitched this same pattern inside the large center square of the square blocks. From there, I used a Frixion marking pen to draw diamond shapes in the light-value squares; four different light-colored squares will meet between each of the blocks (see c). Free motion stitching tiny bubbles inside those diamonds added dimension to the surface.

12. When the quilting is completed, trim the edges of all the quilt layers to be even on all 4 sides, measuring 65 × 78 inches or your desired size.

13. Prepare the binding and bind the quilt following the instructions on page 154.

14. Label your quilt following the instructions on page 156.

13

Taupe

Japanese taupe quilts are a style of patchwork typically made with the muted browns and sepias we normally associate with the color taupe, but they can also include some muted reds, blues, and other colors. The style and palette of these quilts are inspired by the tones of the natural clay soil found in Japan and the way the color changes as it is fired and made into traditional pottery. These pieces incorporate time-honored methods such as using pine ash during the firing process to give the pots the beautiful range of taupe shades. Fabrics inspired by these colors have a depth and complexity that are both modern and traditional at the same time.

Playing with this idea, I thought about the inspiration of colors that compose a favorite painting, the grays and sepias in a cherished old photograph, my grandmother's dishes; any of these could make interesting color palettes. I settled on a collection of my own personal pottery pieces to design a quilt around. There is nothing extraordinary or precious about the pieces I have collected, all from thrift stores, very inexpensively. I just love them. They are used throughout our home in various ways, and their neutral range of blues, whites, and tans work well for our décor.

Further inspiration was gleaned from an afternoon spent purging our closets. Clothes the kids had outgrown or that were designated for the donate pile due to a small stain provided the perfect neutrals to create my own taupe quilt. Knowing last year's clothes have become a quilt to warm us and beautify our home makes for a very satisfying quilt indeed.

The layout of this quilt is based on a traditional Thousand Pyramids patchwork pattern, and I will walk you through sewing triangles together. This quilt will also introduce you to a favorite technique of mine, *trapunto*, which provides an extra layer of batting underneath certain areas of the quilt for added emphasis on the surface of the quilt.

Finished Quilt Size:
54 × 63 inches,
for a throw-sized quilt

Techniques: Piecing triangles, using a template or special ruler,

trapunto quilting, free motion quilting

Fabrics

For the Feature Fabric: Approximately 15 pieces of clothing in your chosen palette or ½ yard each of 15 different colors in quilting weight cotton

For the Backing: 4¼ yards 44-inch-wide quilting cotton. Backing should be least 4 inches larger than your quilt top's total length and width.

For the Binding: ½ yard 44-inch-wide quilting cotton in a coordinating color

Feature Fabric Suggestion: Start by collecting object(s) or piece(s) to inspire your color palette. The possibilities are so fun to consider. Think of a beloved painting, wallpaper in a childhood room, photographs, favorite dishes, the color of Dad's first car, and so on. For color variety in my version, I used 11 shirts and 4 pairs of light to midweight pants. This gave me several beiges, blues, creams, and whites to choose from, with leftover fabric for other projects (like a coordinating pillow).

Other Materials

Low-Loft Cotton Batting: Package of twin-sized batting cut to size. Batting should be at least 4 inches larger than your quilt's length and width.

High-Loft Batting for Trapunto Details: 1 yard (I used Quilter's Dream Puff.)

Equilateral triangle quilting ruler (my favorite is Creative Grids 60-degree equilateral triangle ruler #CGRT60) or the template (page 162)

Template plastic available at quilting and craft stores (optional, if using templates)

My Color and Design Notes

I wanted the color palette of my quilt to be simple. Rather than go for a wide range of colors, I opted for several tones of a few basic colors based on my pottery pieces. As I put things up on the design wall, I decided to add in a simple stripe and plaid, but just a little here and there. I also added in several white shirts (7 in total; we wear a lot of white shirts). There are many variations of white and cream cloth, and using more than one can create interesting effects in your quilts.

Leave out layered details like pockets and avoid bulky fabrics like denim and corduroy. Save those for a less complex pattern, like the simple patchwork pattern of *Sample Box*, page 11, or *Cyanotype*, page 125.

In addition to the subtle color palette, this pattern is all about the triangles, and you will cut plenty of them. I cut my triangles using a Sizzix Big Shot die cutter (see Resources). This tool makes quick work of precision cutting through multiple layers of fabric. But not to worry, these triangles can easily be cut the good old-fashioned way by using the ruler listed or the template provided (page 162).

Triangles have bias edges, which will stretch or distort if handled too aggressively, so cut and sew them with care.

If you use the template included, print it out at full size. Cut it out, glue it onto a piece of template plastic, cut that out, place it on the fabric, and trace around it. The plastic will prevent the template from losing its shape.

For the sewn trapunto details, I turned back to my inspiration pottery for ideas. One of the vases had some stamped flower shapes on the surface, and I decided to add similar flower details on my quilt. This is a fun detail that I encourage you to try on your own quilt.

PREPARE THE FABRICS

1. Refer to the section Preparing Vintage and Secondhand Fabric on page 150 for information on preparing your fabric.

CUT THE TRIANGLES

2. Begin by cutting 4½-inch-wide strips from the clothing using a long quilting ruler. The number of triangles you get from each strip will vary with the length of the strip, so aim for the longest area in order to get as many triangles as possible from each strip. (If you are using a die cutter to cut the triangles, cut 5-inch-wide pieces from the strips. Stack several layers of fabric at a time in the die cutter and follow the instructions that came with your machine.)

3. Using an equilateral triangle ruler, align the 4½-inch line of the ruler with the bottom edge of the strip. Cut out this shape. If you are using the template, you will simply trace around this shape and cut it out.

4. Rotate the ruler 180 degrees, align the 4½-inch line with the top edge of the fabric strip, and cut (see a). If you are using the template, rotate the template 180 degrees, trace, and cut.

5. Repeat this sequence of steps all the way across the strip, cutting as many triangles as you can. (Note: You will have a blunt tip on the triangles if you are cutting with the ruler or template; don't be alarmed that you've cut off the tip of your triangle. This is actually a handy guide for lining up the triangles to sew them together and will make sense soon.)

6. You need a total of 400 triangles in your chosen color range; how you divide this up between the colors you have is up to you.

LAY OUT THE DESIGN

7. Put on some music and start playing with the layout. On a design wall, lay out the triangles following the illustration (see b) for placement, 16 rows of 25 triangles in each row. Be sure to orient the triangles at the beginning of each row correctly, as they set the layout for the row. Step back occasionally and look at the entire design through a reducing glass to see how the colors flow across the quilt top. When you are pleased with the layout, snap a photo to refer to during construction of the quilt.

CONSTRUCT THE QUILT TOP

8. Construct the quilt in rows, beginning from the top left corner. The key to sewing triangles together is carefully lining up the edges and keeping the ¼-inch seam allowance as consistent as possible. If you have a blunt tip on your triangle, once your triangle pieces are lined up, you will have a neat ¼-inch dog-ear point sticking out from the piece positioned underneath. Use these dog-ears to help align your triangles perfectly as you sew (see c).

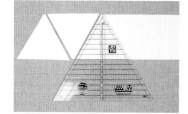

a.

b.

c.

Continue sewing each row together this way, only pressing the row once it is completed. Press the seam allowances for each row in the opposite direction of the one before it, so the seams will nest together and reduce bulk. (Note: As you complete a row, trim away the dog-ears sticking out at the top of each seam to reduce overall bulk in the quilt.)

9. Sew the rows to each other, starting from the top, right sides together. I usually add a pin where each of the points meets up to keep them aligned. This will slow your stitching down, but it helps to line up the points nicely. Sew the rows together, taking care to not chop off any of the points as you sew. Repeat to sew all the rows together. Press the seam allowances between the rows in the same consistent direction.

CREATE THE TRAPUNTO DETAILS ON THE QUILT TOP

If you are not using trapunto, proceed to the next step.

10. To add any sort of trapunto detail, begin by using a Frixion or water-soluble marking pen to draw directly on the right side of the quilt top; these will be the lines on which you will sew. Don't draw anything complicated or small—a simple flower, leaf, or other shape, about the size of your hand, is perfect. Draw a few scattered designs around the patchwork top.

d.

11. Cut a piece of high-loft batting slightly larger than your design and place it directly under the drawing, adding a few pins to secure it. Set your sewing machine up for free motion stitching (refer to Quilting 101, page 153), and begin stitching on the lines you drew, just as if you were free motion quilting. Stitch along the outline of the shapes only; do not fill them in or you will lose the poufy effect of the extra batting. Once you have stitched around the shape, turn the work over and carefully trim away the extra batting that extends beyond the shape (see d). Do this very carefully, so as not to cut into the quilt top. The result is that the inside of the shape is now filled in with an added layer of batting, and this will create extra dimension when the layers are quilted together.

FINISH THE QUILT

Refer to Quilting 101 (page 145) for more information on each of these steps.

12. Piece fabric together to make the quilt backing, which should measure at least 4 inches larger than the finished top's length and width. Layer the quilt backing, batting, and quilt top to create a quilt sandwich of all 3 layers. Pin baste the layers together.

13. Quilt the layers. Begin by free motion quilting around the trapunto shapes from Step 11 at least once to secure them. I actually like the look better when there are multiple stitch lines, as it helps further define the design. If you do several lines, do not worry about retracing the previous stitch lines exactly.

14. Next, choose your free motion quilting design, but there is no need to quilt over the trapunto shapes again. I chose to do all loopy free motion design over the entire quilt, which helped to add more dimension to the flowers I drew (see b).

15. When you are finished quilting, square up the edges of the quilt to be 54 × 63 inches or your desired size. Trim away half of the triangles along the two long edges of the quilt (see b).

16. Prepare the binding and bind the quilt following the instructions on page 154.

17. Label your quilt following the instructions on page 156.

14

Leaving the Nest

I got a little sentimental while creating this quilt. I was thinking about my oldest child leaving for college at some point, which will be happening sooner than I care to realize. (In fact, when you read this, she may already be there!) We parents all know the inevitability of our children growing up and moving on. We've prepared them for it, maybe better than we've prepared ourselves. As a quilt maker, I could not, in good conscience, let a child leave home without a handmade quilt, in particular a quilt made of fabrics and reminders of home to help them continue their story in a new place.

However, I wasn't quite ready to make her "leaving-the-nest quilt." Instead I made a practice version with a collection of beautiful vintage Marimekko fabrics I have. I chose them for their bold colors and large, graphic patterns. This quilt is made of classic flying geese blocks, which seems very fitting for the child who must find his or her own wings and fly. Enlarging the geese units is a great way to use large prints and create a more graphic and modern design.

Finished Quilt Size:
72 × 66 inches,
for a throw- or twin-sized quilt

Finished Block Size:
12 × 6 inches

Techniques: Making large Flying Geese units, free motion quilting using an all-over stencil design, using large prints

Fabrics

For the Feature Fabric: 3¾ yards total of a variety of fabric with large patterns for the geese

For the Top: 4¼ yards 44-inch-wide quilting cotton for the background

For the Backing: 4½ yards 44-inch-wide quilting cotton. Backing should be least 4 inches larger than your quilt top's total length and width.

For the Binding: ½ yard 44-inch-wide quilting cotton in a coordinating color for the binding

Feature Fabric Suggestion: I used 24 vintage Marimekko cotton remnants in various sizes. Any light to midweight cotton with a large print is great for this design.

Other Materials

Low-Loft Cotton Batting: Package of twin-sized batting cut to size. Batting should be at least 4 inches larger than your quilt's total length and width.

Clamshell Quilting Stencil (Optional; I used #272 Clamshell from Quilting Creations.)

My Color and Design Notes

In my opinion, you can't really go wrong with iconic Marimekko prints. I knew I wanted good contrast between the "geese" and the "sky" units to clearly define the overall pattern and create a very graphic feel. However, it would be just as beautiful to create this design in a subtle palette.

By enlarging these Flying Geese blocks, I could feature more of the large prints. This pattern would also work well with solids and small print fabrics. You could also use bulkier fabrics, such as corduroy or wool, as the feature fabrics.

I used a very soft gray for the background, reminiscent of our Seattle skies. It helps the whites within the prints pop and creates nice depth around the bold prints.

The prints themselves were all sizes, some very large. By using a clear quilter's ruler as a sort of viewfinder and moving it around the print before cutting, I was able to determine which areas showed the printed pattern best.

I used a premade quilting stencil with an overall clamshell design to mark the quilt top for free motion quilting. The clamshell is a very fun shape to stitch— and forgiving and quick.

PREPARE THE FABRIC

Refer to the section Preparing Vintage and Secondhand Fabric on page 150 for information on preparing your fabric.

CUT THE FABRICS

1. Cut 12½ × 6½-inch rectangles from the printed fabrics. These are used for the triangle center (goose) of each block. A total of 66 are needed.

2. From the background (sky) fabric, cut 6½-inch strips across the width of the solid quilting cotton. (Tip: To make this step easier, fold the yardage in half widthwise, selvedge to selvedge, lining up the fold along a straight line on the bottom of your cutting mat [the fold is positioned closest to you]. Establish a straight edge on one side, then from that edge, measure and cut 6½-inch-wide strips through both layers.) You'll need 22 strips.

3. Sub cut the strips into 6½-inch squares. With careful cutting, you should be able to get 6 squares from each strip. A total of 132 squares are needed.

MAKE THE FLYING GEESE UNITS

4. To make a Flying Geese unit, position one 12½ × 6½-inch goose rectangle right side up on your worktable. Lay one 6½ × 6½-inch sky square over the right side of the rectangle, wrong side up, lining up the cut edges. Using a pencil and a ruler, measure and draw a line on the sky square from the top left corner diagonally to the bottom right corner. This is your sewing line. Stitch through both fabrics along that line. Once sewn, use a ruler and rotary cutter to measure ¼ inch away from the stitched line on the side closest to the top right corner. Cut away all but ¼-inch seam allowance. Press the seam allowance toward the solid fabric. (Note: It is important to press between attaching the corner pieces to help create a nice top point.) Repeat this step on the other side of the rectangle, drawing the diagonal line from the top right corner of the solid square to the bottom left corner. Stitch along that line, trim away the excess seam allowance, and press the seam allowances toward the solid fabric. This creates 1 Flying Geese block. The completed unit should have ¼ inch of solid fabric extending beyond the top point at the join to prevent the

a.

point from being cut off when the units are sewn together (see a). Square up each block and, if necessary, trim to measure 12½ × 6½ inches. You will need a total of 66 units.

LAY OUT THE DESIGN

5. On a design wall or cleared space, arrange the Flying Geese blocks in 11 rows of 6 blocks each, using the illustration (see b) as a guide. In my quilt, every other linear column of geese is flying in the opposite direction, but you may prefer to position yours differently. Once the layout feels right, snap a picture of it to refer to later.

CONSTRUCT THE QUILT TOP

6. I constructed this quilt in columns. Starting at the top left block and moving down the column, sew each of the blocks to each other, wrong sides together. (Tip: When sewing 2 blocks together, I find it helpful to position the block with the point of the goose unit on top when I sew. This allows me to see it as I sew across the top of the point and not cut it off.) Press all the seam allowances of each column away from the points of the geese.

7. Sew the columns to each other, starting from the left. I find it helpful to add a pin where the seams meet to help line things up. Press all the seam allowances to the same side.

FINISH THE QUILT

Refer to Quilting 101 (page 145) for more information on each of these steps.

8. As needed, piece fabric together to make the quilt backing, which should measure at least 4 inches larger than the finished top's length and width. Layer the quilt backing, batting, and quilt top to create a quilt sandwich of all 3 layers. Pin baste the layers together.

9. Quilt the layers. I used a Frixion pen to trace the all-over clamshell stencil design on my quilt. I free motion stitched the design, following the drawn lines loosely and using a thread that coordinated to the background sky fabric. I stitched these from the center of the quilt working out to the edge, then flipped the quilt around and stitched the other half from the center to the edge, but upside down. This switch prevents having to shove a lot of quilt layers in the harp space of your sewing machine.

10. When you are finished quilting, square up the edges of the quilt to be 72 × 66 inches or your desired size.

11. Prepare the binding and bind the quilt following the instructions on page 154.

12. Label your quilt following the instructions on page 156.

b.

15

Muumuu

Traditional Hawaiian muumuus are loose-fitting dresses, most often printed in brightly colored, cheery floral patterns. Growing up in the southeastern United States, the women in my family wore housecoats, which are very similar to muumuus, so I have a strong association with this domestic "uniform" and the idea of cooking, relaxing with loved ones, and being at home. When I decided to explore Hawaiian quilting, I chose a vintage muumuu from my collection as my fabric muse. It is made of a bright blue, pink, and yellow floral print, and it exemplifies comfort and ease in my mind, just like those housecoats worn by the women from my childhood.

Hawaiian quilting has a distinctively different look than traditional patchwork but is equally beautiful and fun to try. The base for the quilt top is normally one piece of cloth, instead of pieced patchwork. On top of the base cloth is a symmetrical fabric motif, cut from folded fabric, paper snowflake style, and hand appliquéd onto the base cloth. Traditional motifs were inspired by the lush plant life of the climate, but today everything goes.

If you are new to needle-turn appliqué, do not be afraid to try it on a treasured dress or some other textile you want to feature. I designed this wall hanging project to be a manageable size and portable. You might be surprised at how satisfying and relaxing this type of "slow stitching" handwork can be.

Finished Quilt Size:
20 × 40 inches,
for a wall hanging

Finished Block Size:
20 × 20 inches

Techniques: Needle-turn
appliqué, cutting fabric using
templates, hand quilting, making
a quilt sleeve

Fabrics

For the Feature Fabric: Two 15-inch squares cut from a vintage muumuu, beloved dress, or some other vividly patterned textile or ½ yard of quilting cotton fabric

For the Top: ¾ yard 44-inch-wide quilting cotton fabric

For the Backing: 1⅝ yards 44-inch-wide quilting cotton. Backing should be least 4 inches larger than your quilt top's total length and width.

For the Binding: ¾ yard 44-inch-wide quilting cotton in a coordinating color

For the Hanging Sleeve: 8½ × 20-inch piece of fabric in a coordinating color

Feature Fabric Suggestion: The muumuu I used is vintage 1970s, so I had fun creating a color palette that reflected that. Regardless of the colors you choose, it's best to have strong contrast between the background fabric and the dress fabric so that your appliqué motif pops.

Other Materials

Low-Loft Cotton Batting: 1 package of craft-sized batting cut to size. Batting should be at least 4 inches larger than your quilt's length and width.

Appliqué Template, page 163 (optional)

22-inch-wide wooden dowel, for hanging

My Color and Design Notes

I wanted this piece to have some color and pattern drama because it was a smaller piece and would be hung on the wall. Like a special piece of artwork or picture, you may want your quilt to have a little drama (or not, you decide) or coordinate with your furnishings. Consider where the piece will hang and what would be fun to see on it. The size of this appliqué is perfect for a fun, larger-scale print.

I will walk you through the steps of cutting out the appliqué piece, which is a lot like making a paper snowflake, as well as my favorite method of needle-turn appliqué.

The template for my appliqué motif is included on page 163, but if you decide to create your own design, keep the shapes simple. Gentle curves and minimal sharp angles will be more successful (and enjoyable) to stitch.

In needle-turn appliqué, the edges of the motif are turned under by about ¼ inch as they are hand stitched onto the base cloth, but there's no need to stress over being exact about this. It's much easier than it sounds.

Some fabrics can have a tendency to fray at the edges, making it harder to turn under and manipulate them during appliqué. A bit of fray block brushed at the edges of the fabric will prevent fraying and make it more manageable. (See Quilting 101, page 145.)

Using appliqué glue to hold the fabric in place is simple to do and creates a strong, water-soluble, temporary hold with just a tiny dot (the size of a pinhead is all you need). Gluing is my preferred way to baste. Apply it and allow five minutes to dry. The piece can then be folded up and carried off without worry of it coming apart. Also, there's no getting stuck with pins.

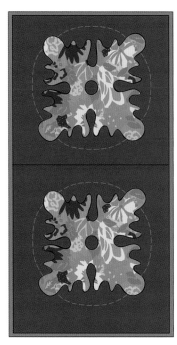

a.

b.

c.

PREPARE THE FABRICS

1. Refer to the section Preparing Vintage and Secondhand Fabric on page 150 for information on preparing your fabric.

CUT THE BACKGROUND FABRIC

2. Cut two 20½-inch squares. Set aside.

PREPARE THE APPLIQUÉ FABRIC

3. If you are using the template provided, print it out at full size and cut it out. To create your own template instead, do the following: Cut a 15-inch square from newspaper. Fold it in half once, then fold it in half again so that it is completely folded into quarters. Last, fold it in half diagonally aligning all unfolded edges on the same side. Sketch out a simple design and cut out, similar to making a paper snowflake.

4. Fold each square of your feature fabric evenly into quarters to mark the center. Set the folds by lightly pressing them with an iron, and keep the fabric folded for the next step.

5. Lay the paper template over one of the folded fabric squares, lining up the edge of the template with the folded edge of your fabric as indicated on the template. Pin it in place. Trace the template design onto the fabric using a Frixion or water-soluble marking pen, and remove the template. Cut the traced design out with fabric scissors, cutting through all the layers of fabric. Repeat this step for the other square. You'll need 2 identical appliqué motifs from your feature fabric.

CONSTRUCT THE QUILT TOP

6. Fold a 20½-inch square of backing fabric into quarters and finger press a crease to mark the center. Place the cut appliqué motif, right side up, on the base fabric, also right side up, using the pressed lines of both to center the motif on the background fabric. Add a few pins to temporarily hold everything in place (see a).

7. Peel back 1 corner of the appliqué motif, add a tiny dot of appliqué glue to the back in a couple of places (stay at least 1 inch away from the edges), and smooth the motif back into place (see b). Repeat this step for all 4 symmetrical sides of the design. Add a dot or two of glue to the very center of the motif as well. Repeat this step for the second piece of backing fabric and appliqué motif.

8. Before beginning to stitch, it may be helpful to turn under the edges ¼ inch and pinch the fold with your fingers to crease it, then stitch that crease down as you sew. Using a Milliner or small quilting-sized needle and a thread color that coordinates with the feature/appliqué motif fabric, start the first appliqué stitch at an area of the motif with a larger outside curve. Bring the needle up from the back of the base fabric. Directly where you will take the next stitch, sweep the raw edge of the appliqué motif under ¼ inch. Take a small stitch to secure it in place. Continue stitching all the way around the piece (see c). At tight curves, make a few small clips into the seam allowance as you sweep it under with your needle. This stitching becomes more rhythmic as you get going: sweep the fabric under, stitch, sweep the fabric under, stitch. Appliqué both motifs to the background blocks using this method.

9. Press and sew the 2 blocks together using a ¼-inch seam, and press the seam allowance to one side.

FINISH THE QUILT

Refer to Quilting 101 (page 145) for more information on each of these steps.

10. Piece fabric together, if needed, to make the quilt backing, which should measure at least 4 inches larger than the finished top's length and width. Layer the quilt backing, batting, and quilt top to create a quilt sandwich of all 3 layers. Pin baste the layers together.

11. Hand quilt the layers. Hoop your quilt if using a quilting hoop. Using size 8 Perle cotton thread, quilt a running stitch outlining the outside of the appliqué, about ¼ to ½ inch away from the edge of the appliqué (see d). I also hand quilted a circle around each motif, which I marked by tracing around a large bowl with a marking pen (see a).

d.

12. When you are finished quilting, square up the edges of the quilt to be 20 × 40 inches or your desired size.

13. Prepare the binding and bind the quilt following the instructions on page 154.

14. Label your quilt following the instructions on page 156.

15. Create the hanging sleeve following the instructions on page 157.

16

Hand Stitched

As practical as the modern sewing machine is, I will always love the analog aspect of hand sewing. Stitching by hand requires slowing down, something we don't seem to do enough of these days. As I settle into a project, my hands develop their own rhythm, and it can feel quite meditative. I've worked on my English paper piecing (EPP) skills over the past few years, and I have found it to be the perfect technique to get cozy with after a long day. The supplies needed are few, and I keep mine in a small tin box that I can throw in my bag to stitch on the go. I love that I can take advantage of those otherwise wasted moments.

Small fabric bits and precious scraps—this project is perfect for all those little pieces you hang on to because you love them but can't use because they are perhaps too small for most projects. If you have enough fabric to wrap around the paper template, you have all you need. This project is small enough to complete in a weekend.

For this framed piece, I used a collection of coveted Liberty of London Tana Lawn cotton prints. Each one of these iconic classic prints is like a little piece of art, distinctively British and full of color. Constructed entirely by hand, EPP is the process of basting scraps of fabric around pieces of paper and then sewing them together.

Finished Quilt Size:
15 × 15 inches (unframed),
for framed art

Techniques: English paper
piecing, creating design from
color value

Fabrics

For the Feature Fabric: Scraps of special fabrics

Feature Fabric Suggestion: I used 40 different prints of Liberty of London Tana Lawn cottons. You can use any group of fabrics with a variety of color and pattern.

Other Materials

English paper piecing templates (see note below)

Twenty 1½-inch honeycombs

Sixteen 1⁷⁄₁₆-inch 8-petal chrysanthemums

Eight 1½-inch squares

One 1-inch hexagon

20 × 20-inch picture frame

Mat board in coordinating color, cut to fit inside frame

Four spacers to fit inside the perimeter of the frame, to allow room between the glass and the piece

Awl to poke a hole through the mat board

Note: Paper piecing templates are available as a prepackaged kit through PaperPieces.com and at wisecrafthandmade.com. Just search for "Wise Craft Handstitched OCT100."

My Color and Design Notes

This piece plays with the light and dark color value of the fabrics, and it is best to start with more scraps than you need, paring down your choices as the design develops. Other ways to create a design could be achieved by sorting your fabrics by color or pattern. Anything that can create some sort of discernable pattern you find pleasing would work.

Keep in mind the paper templates are not removed from the back of the pieces, so you will need the full quantities indicated for different shapes. There are prepackaged kits available made of acid-free paper; see "Other Materials."

There is more than one way to baste the fabrics to the templates in EPP. I prefer glue basting with a glue pen made for fabric (see Quilting 101 on page 145), which is the method I will explain here. Use any method you prefer; the results are the same.

The EPP technique is perfect for "fussy cutting," which refers to intentionally cutting out a certain motif of the fabric in order to feature it in that piece.

Once an EPP project is complete, usually the paper pieces are removed. Because this is a hanging piece, we'll leave the paper pieces in, which allows the piece to sit flatter in the frame.

PREPARE THE FABRICS

1. Refer to the section Preparing Vintage and Secondhand Fabric on page 150 for information on preparing your fabric.

BASTE THE FABRICS TO THE PAPER PIECES

You will need a rough idea of which fabrics will be used with which paper piecing shapes before starting to baste. Use the finished photo and illustration (see a) for reference. (Tip: I played around until I found a rough layout I liked and snapped a photo of it to refer to while I basted.)

2. To baste fabric to paper, roughly cut a piece of fabric ¼ inch larger than the paper piece it will be basted to. (Note: no need for exact cutting. Just allow enough fabric to wrap around to the back of the paper.) Center the paper piece on the wrong side of the fabric. Working on the back of the paper template, apply glue along one edge of the paper. Wrap the fabric to the back of the paper, allowing the glue to hold it down. Repeat on all edges of the paper template, folding all the corner edges neatly toward the back and securing them. Be sure that the fabric on the front of the template is pulled taut but not tight, and the edges are smooth and crisp. Do this for all 45 paper templates and fabrics needed.

LAY OUT THE DESIGN

3. Lay out the pieces following the illustration (see a). Starting from the center of the design, I alternated light and dark values as I moved outward. Fitting the pieces is a bit like putting together a puzzle. Once you settle on a design you like, take a picture to refer to as you work.

HAND SEW THE PIECES TOGETHER

4. Using coordinating neutral thread and a hand-sewing needle, stitch the design together starting from the center octagon piece and moving outward. To stitch 2 pieces together, place them right sides together, lining up the edges to be sewn. Using blind stitches, sew along the edge, being careful not to sew through the paper. Take an extra stitch at the corners for added stability. If you can continue stitching on another piece without breaking your thread, keep going. Periodically check your work from the front to be sure your stitches are not too big—the goal is to not see the stitches (see b). (Note: If I look closely at mine, some stitches are barely visible. I actually don't mind seeing a bit of the maker's hand.)

5. Even though you are not removing the paper from the individual pieces as you sew, you will at times need to bend the paper pieces slightly during the sewing process. That is okay. Just do not fold or put a hard crease in them.

6. Continue stitching the pieces together, moving outward in the design, until all the pieces are sewn together.

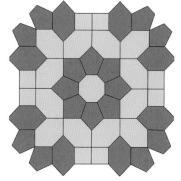

a.

b.

PRESS AND FRAME THE PIECE

7. Likely your piece may need a pressing before framing. Use a dry, hot iron and cover the work with a press cloth. Thoroughly press it flat from both sides.

8. To frame the piece, begin by finding the horizontal and vertical center of the mat board. Carefully center the piece on the mat board, top to bottom and side to side. Hold it in place temporarily with small pieces of tape on the back of the piece, if needed.

9. I found the best way to secure the piece was to sew it to the mat board with an inconspicuous stitch at each corner and in the very middle, going straight through the mat board. Use an awl to pierce a hole through the mat board where the stitches will be made. Use a tapestry needle with a sharp point and thread that will blend in with the piece. Bring the needle up from the back of the mat board through the guide hole to the front. Make sure you are sewing through all the layers with a small stitch that is hidden (in a join between 2 pieces is a good area), and bring the needle back in and to the back of the art board, through the same guide hole. Knot the thread several times to secure it to the back of the mat board; add a dot of glue at the knot if desired, for extra stability. Repeat this step everywhere you want to secure your piece to the mat board.

10. Attach the 4 spacer bars inside the perimeter of your frame to allow space between your needlework and the glass.

11. Finally, insert the matted piece into the frame. Hang and admire your beautiful hand stitched work.

17

Medallion

Barkcloth fabric was at the height of its popularity in the 1940s, '50s, and '60s and was commonly used in home furnishings like curtains and upholstery. Its nubby surface texture and characteristic bold floral prints, colorful tropical imagery, and midcentury motifs make it an easy fabric to spot at secondhand stores. So many of us have fond memories tied up in barkcloth prints—perhaps it was used for our grandmother's curtains or to cover a sofa we sat on as a child, or maybe it reminds us of a family vacation we went on.

I was given a collection of vintage barkcloth fabrics and other similar fabrics by my friend Cathi Bessell-Browne, creator and designer of *Gertrude Made*. She designs beautiful dresses from these fabrics, and I was more than happy to put her scraps to good use in a quilt. The quilt I planned would be used in an otherwise neutral guest room, creating just the jolt of color that room needed. I picked up a cotton bedsheet in a mustard shade at the thrift store to cut up and used it with the barkcloth to create a pattern of asymmetrical triangles that would radiate from the quilt's center. This type of design is called "medallion." I wanted to have areas in a secondary pattern of solid color in the midst of the bright patchwork pattern, because the array of patterns and colors is more clearly discernable if there is another pattern happening around them; otherwise, it just all jumbles together. I was so happy with this quilt—and even went so far as to quilt it in a diamond grid pattern, reminiscent of those quilted, Barbie-bright robes and bedspreads from my childhood.

Finished Quilt Size:
65 × 91 inches,
for a twin-sized quilt

Finished Block Size:
6½ × 6½ inches

Techniques: Improvisational
piecing by adding triangle
shapes to square blocks,
walking foot quilting

Fabrics

For the Feature Fabric: Barkcloth fabrics in a variety
of colors, about 5 total yards

For the Top: One twin-sized vintage sheet or 1 yard
44-inch-wide quilting cotton in a solid color to form the
medallion pattern

For the Backing: 6 yards 44-inch-wide quilting cotton
fabric. Backing should be least 4 inches larger than
your quilt top's total length and width.

For the Binding: ¾ yard 44-inch-wide quilting cotton
in a coordinating solid color

Feature Fabric Suggestion: Try to collect a large
variety of barkcloth prints. I used 25 different colors/
prints. The size of each of the fabrics should allow for
at least four or five 7-inch squares to be cut from them.
The smaller the fabric scraps, the more fabrics you
will need. The quilt requires one hundred forty 7-inch
squares. Also suitable are feedsack printed cottons,
calicos, or even all solids for a very modern quilt.

Other Materials

Low-Loft Cotton Batting: Package of full-sized batting cut to size. Backing should be least 4 inches larger
than your quilt top's length and width.

My Color and Design Notes

The key to creating a vibrant quilt full of color is variety.
Do not hoard your favorite fabrics. This is the quilt to
use them in. I found using a combination of both vibrant
bright prints and slightly calmer prints worked well in
the overall design. Using only bright prints would have
been too much.

If you simply do not have enough of a favorite print to
squeeze out a 7-inch square, you can intentionally make
that one a part of the medallion design (since those
squares will have parts cut from them anyway) or piece
it with a similar print to create a 7-inch square. I love
adding details like this to my quilts.

Use a fresh blade in your rotary cutter, as these fabrics
are a bit heavier than regular quilting cottons.

You should lay out the entire design before creating the
improvisational "snowball" blocks for the center medallion pattern. It is important that the overall design be
decided on before creating the secondary design. Use a
reducing glass to look at the overall design.

The hot pink I chose for the binding was meant to contrast and frame the quilt. One of the things I love about
quilt making is the way clashing or disparate fabrics can
suddenly feel connected and meant to be side by side
when framed with binding. It visually holds them all in,
and deciding if yours will blend or contrast with the quilt
is an important design decision.

PREPARE THE FABRIC

1. Refer to the section Preparing Vintage and Secondhand Fabric on page
150 for information on preparing your fabric.

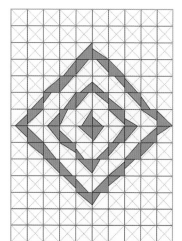

a.

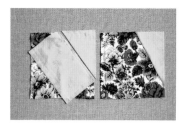

b.

CUT SQUARES FROM THE BARKCLOTH

2. From each of the barkcloth fabrics, cut as many 7 × 7-inch squares as you can. You will need a total of 140 squares.

LAY OUT THE DESIGN

3. Settle on a placement of the barkcloth prints before you begin creating the center medallion design. Lay out the squares on a design wall following the illustration (see a), creating 14 rows of 10 squares each. I had no real plan to the order I placed my squares. I put them up quickly, then later spent some time moving them around to create a layout I liked. Once you settle on a design that appeals to you, take a picture to refer to as you work.

CREATE THE MEDALLION PATTERN

4. From the solid sheet, cutting edge to edge, cut a strip 7 inches wide. Sub cut the strip into rectangles of varying sizes—some can be almost 7 inches, some much narrower. A total of 60 rectangles are needed.

5. Remove the 4 barkcloth squares at the very center of the layout from your design wall. These will be used to create the center of the medallion. Lay 1 square on the worktable, right side up. Lay 1 solid rectangle, right side up, on top of 1 side of the square. (Note: It doesn't matter which side, but I always position it on the right side of the square out of habit.) The rectangle should cover 2 adjacent edges of the barkcloth square. It should also extend beyond the edges of the barkcloth by at least ¼ inch to ensure that the finished square can be trimmed to the correct size (see b).

6. Once you decide where the rectangle will be positioned, flip it over, keeping it in position to sew, so that right sides of both fabrics are together (see b). Stitch them together. Trim the excess barkcloth under the rectangle to ¼ inch (be sure to trim this away from the side of the stitch line closest to the corner edge) and press the seam allowances toward the solid fabric. Check that the square measures 7 × 7 inches, and trim any excess fabric away. Repeat this step with the other 3 squares to create the 4 squares needed for the medallion pattern, but vary the angle of the solid square on every block so that each resulting block looks a little bit different. This technique creates the improvisational look.

7. Place the 4 center squares back up on the design wall. Create the next ring of the medallion pattern the same way: remove the appropriate squares from the wall, add the rectangles and trim as described in step 6, then put the squares back up on the design wall following the illustration for how these new blocks are positioned in the design. You will need a total of 60 of these improvisational squares to complete the medallion design. Once you finish adding the solid squares, take a picture to refer to as you work.

CONSTRUCT THE QUILT TOP

8. Sew the quilt top together in rows, starting from the top left and going across. There are 14 rows of 10 blocks each. Press each row's seam allowances in the opposite direction so the seams will nest and line up when the rows are sewn together.

9. Sew the rows together, starting from the top. I usually add a pin where each of the seams meet to line everything up. Continue until all 14 rows are sewn. Press all the seam allowances to the same side.

FINISH THE QUILT

Refer to Quilting 101 (page 145) for more information on each of these steps.

10. Piece fabric together, if needed, to make the quilt backing, which should measure at least 4 inches larger than the finished top's length and width. Layer the quilt backing, batting, and quilt top to create a quilt sandwich of all 3 layers. Pin baste the layers together.

11. Quilt the layers. I used a walking foot fitted on my sewing machine and quilted simple diagonal lines going through every square, in both directions. The diamond pattern I created across the quilt using soft yellow thread seemed to blend with all the different prints best. Mark guidelines for straight lines using a ruler and a marking pen or by laying down painter's blue tape on the quilt top, one line at a time.

12. When you are finished quilting, square up the edges of the quilt to be 65 × 91 inches or your desired size.

13. Prepare the binding and bind the quilt following the instructions on page 154.

14. Label your quilt following the instructions on page 156.

18

Tagged

Sometimes, it's not about the significance of a fabric collection but the creative way it is used. There is just something I have always loved about the serene, pastoral, and sometimes fussy images in toile prints, and I knew the pieces I've collected would make a fun quilt. The prints themselves are not significant to my own life, aside from being a favorite.

Toile does not seem hard to find, and I bring it home to add to my fabric collection all the time. I often pick up fabric remnants and clothing with toile prints when I'm thrift shopping and keep an eye out online for out-of-date upholstery samples (which is how I found the samples for the *Sample Box* quilt, page 11).

Look at one of these fabrics for more than a few seconds, and I bet you can start to see where I went with this quilt. Captioning what the lavishly dressed lords, ladies, and children depicted in the scenes with embroidered details and speech bubbles of things that might be said in your own family can add a fun dimension of humor and endearment to toile squares. Those are the details that make them part of a new story, yours. I sent a batch of toile squares to my sister-in-law Jennifer to embroider, and it was like Christmas morning when I got them back. They were embroidered, embellished, and captioned with the perfect amount of humor. This truly unique quilt is best used in a part of the house where it will elicit conversations and stories.

Finished Quilt Size:
52 × 54 inches for a
throw-sized quilt

Techniques: Hand embroidery,
improvisational piecing, adding a
flange trim on binding

Fabrics

For the Feature Fabric: Approximately 20 toile fabrics in various sizes

For the Backing: 3¾ yards 44-inch-wide quilting cotton fabric. Backing should be least 4 inches larger than your quilt top's total length and width.

For the Flange Trim: ¼ yard 44-inch-wide quilting cotton in a contrasting solid color

For the Binding: ½ yard 44-inch-wide quilting cotton in a coordinating solid color

Feature Fabric Suggestion: I began this project with a collection of about 20 different large and small toile prints I had collected over a period of time, mainly from thrift stores. Some pieces were larger remnants, some were panels I had cut from clothing, and others were small squares that only showed a small part of the print. All of these will work for this project. Keep in mind that you will be embroidering around the images, so larger prints with open space between the images are ideal. Upholstery or home décor weight is best, but quilting weight cottons will work too with a backing of interfacing.

Other Materials

Ultra lightweight fusible interfacing for lightweight fabrics, optional (I used Pellon #12005096.)

Several colors of embroidery thread (I used DMC floss.)

Embroidery hoop

Embroidery needle

Low-Loft Cotton Batting: Package of twin-sized batting cut to size. Batting should be least 4 inches larger than your quilt top's total length and width.

My Color and Design Notes

Keep in mind that embroidery stitches do not need to completely cover the guide marks you draw; those will disappear on their own or with an iron. No one will know you didn't quite hit the line.

Embroidery floss consists of 6 strands twisted together. I typically separate these into 2 lengths of 3 strands each, which is what I used for this project. Use as many strands of floss as you need to make the stitches clear and have good contrast to the background.

It's completely okay to leave some of the toile panels without embroidery; it will keep the overall effect from feeling too cluttered.

If you are using quilting weight cottons, add fusible lightweight interfacing on the wrong side of the fabric before embroidering. This keeps the embroidery floss on the back from showing through to the front.

The contrast flange trim peeking out from the binding is a fun touch and a nice place to pick up on one of the bright embroidery thread colors. Actually, this is a nice detail to add to any quilt that has traditional binding.

PREPARE THE FABRIC

1. Refer to the section Preparing Vintage and Secondhand Fabric on page 150 for information on preparing your fabric.

2. Add lightweight, fusible interfacing to the back of any lighter or quilting weight fabrics to keep the embroidery floss from showing through. Follow the manufacturer's instructions. Cut a piece roughly the size of the fabric piece (maybe slightly smaller so you won't fuse it to your ironing board) and place it glue side down on the back of the fabric. Cover everything with a press cloth and iron the stack to fuse the interfacing to the back of the fabric.

ROUGH CUT SQUARES OF TOILE TO EMBROIDER

3. I found it helpful to use a 14-inch square ruler over my fabric to act as a viewfinder and help me decide where I would "fussy cut" images from larger pieces of fabric. Make sure your cuts include some space around the scene to add captioning, as well as an extra ¼-inch seam allowance on all 4 sides. This quilt is pieced together in big blocks, sort of like fitting a puzzle together, so the blocks don't need to be the same size. In fact, I think it's much better if they aren't.

EMBROIDER THE SQUARES

4. Consider sending some squares off to friends or family members, asking them to embroider a square and contribute to the quilt.

5. With a Frixion or water-soluble marking pen, draw or write what you plan to embroider directly on the right side of the fabric to guide you as you stitch. Place your fabric into an embroidery hoop. Use the marks as a rough guide for the embroidery stitches. To create a backstitch for the letters, bring the needle up from the back of the fabric to make a single stitch along the drawn line. Insert the needle about ¼ inch away, on the line. Take the next stitch, coming up from the back again, ¼ inch ahead of the last stitch. Insert the needle back at the end of the previous stitch to finish the stitch (hence, the name *backstitch*). Continue doing this for all the letters. Also consider filling in some of the print with different embroidery stitches, adding small details here and there. Embroider as many of the fabrics/blocks as you wish before moving on to the next step.

LAY OUT THE DESIGN

6. Much like the *Boro* coverlet (page 41), putting the blocks together is a very improvisational process. On a design wall or cleared space, arrange the blocks using the illustration (see a) only as a rough guide. I started with my favorite blocks for the center of the quilt, putting them up in the center area of the design wall. Place a few fabrics around those center ones, stepping back

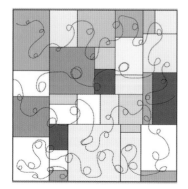

a.

and looking at the design from time to time, and continuing to add. Distribute similar colors and blocks across the quilt. Do not worry about orienting all the toile images in the same direction. They should be turned in all directions, as that is how a quilt is used and enjoyed. Once the layout feels right, snap a picture of it to refer to later.

CONSTRUCT THE QUILT TOP

7. Start by sewing the center pieces together. Choose 2 blocks that are roughly the same size, sew them together, press the seam allowances to one side, and trim 1 edge straight for adding the next blocks. If the next blocks are too small, sew other blocks to them until they are an appropriate size, then add them to the center blocks (see b). Piece another set of blocks, adding those to the previous blocks unit, perhaps orienting the prints in different directions. Press the seam allowances to one side.

b.

8. Continue piecing until your quilt top measures at least 52 × 54 inches. If needed, trim the sides of the quilt to square up the edges.

FINISH THE QUILT

Refer to Quilting 101 (page 145) for more information on each of these steps.

9. Piece fabric together, if needed, to make the quilt backing, which should measure at least 4 inches larger than the finished top's length and width. Layer the quilt backing, batting, and quilt top to create a quilt sandwich of all 3 layers. Pin baste the layers together.

10. Quilt the layers. I didn't want the quilting I did to take attention away from the embroidery, only add texture. I settled on a free motion loop-d-loop design in a coordinating cream thread done all over the quilt top, even stitching over the embroidered captions. This is a quick way to free motion quilt and unifies the entire design.

11. When you are finished quilting, square up the edges of the quilt to be 52 × 54 inches or your desired size.

CREATE THE FLANGE TRIM

12. To create a flange trim, cut six 2½-inch-wide strips from the ¼-yard fabric chosen for the flange. Sew these strips together end to end to create 1 continuous length. Press the strip in half, wrong sides together, lengthwise. (To join the strips, follow the Quilting 101 section on binding, steps 2 and 3. It is the same method.)

13. To sew the flange trim to the quilt, start at a corner edge of the quilt, on the front. Align the raw edge of the trim with the edge of the quilt. Sew the flange trim down using a scant ¼-inch seam allowance, backstitching at the beginning. It is very helpful to use a walking foot for this step to pull all the

c.

layers through the sewing process evenly, but a patchwork foot will work in a pinch. When you reach the end of the first side, take a backstitch, remove the quilt and flange from under the presser foot, trim the flange binding to be flush with the edge of the quilt. Turn the quilt 45 degrees, reposition the length of flange on the quilt top, and begin sewing down the side (see c). Repeat on all 4 sides.

14. Prepare the binding and bind the quilt following the instructions on page 154. The goal is to cover the stitching line from the flange trim, so be sure to use a full ¼-inch seam allowance to attach the binding.

15. Label your quilt following the instructions on page 156.

19

Cyanotype

The pages of drawings and attempts at writing my children did when they were small are precious to me. As my son was more drawn to imaginative play in his early childhood, there are only a few bits of drawings done by him, which I've fortunately saved. My daughter was the complete opposite; her first love has always been drawing and art, and she is very talented. The sheer volume of her early sketches and drawings is mind-blowing, but just as precious.

How could I create a quilt of special keepsakes from all these random bits of paper and favorite childhood themes? Cyanotype, or sun printing, is a beautiful way to preserve these sweet mementos of childhood—drawings, maps, or any of those early letters and written words. Cyanotypes were originally used to make copies of architect's blueprints, so with care it is possible to pick up small type and written words very clearly. Part of the beauty of this sun-printed quilt is its simplicity, allowing the maker to include non-sewers in the family to help create it. Gather artwork, written stories, and favorite childhood toys and have fun experimenting. The sun does the work, and the sewing steps are minimal. The beautiful blue shade of the finished fabric will work in any décor.

Pretreated cyanotype fabric comes ready to use right out of the package, and by printing artwork out on clear transparency sheets first, you can get a very clear, crisp print.

Finished Quilt Size:
64 × 80 inches,
for a twin-sized quilt

Finished Block Size:
8 × 8 inches

Techniques: Printing on fabric,
easy square patchwork construction, walking foot quilting

Fabrics

For the Feature Fabric: Eighty 8½-inch squares pretreated cyanotype quilting weight cotton

For the Backing: 6 yards 44-inch-wide quilting cotton
fabric. Backing should be least 4 inches larger than
your quilt top's total length and width.

For the Binding: ½ yard 44-inch-wide quilting cotton
in a coordinating color

Feature Fabric Suggestion: I used 4 packages of Blueprints on Fabric, which comes in a pack of 20 precut,
pretreated 8½-inch squares, available from Dharma
Trading

Other Materials

Objects to Print: Consider children's artwork, poetry
and stories they've written, a favorite small toy, silhouettes, and photos

Computer, printer, and scanner

Package of letter-sized printable transparency film
sheets suitable for your printer (available at most office
supply stores)

Black permanent marker

Low-Loft Cotton Batting: Package of twin-sized batting cut to size. Batting should be least 4 inches larger
than your quilt top's total length and width.

My Color and Design Notes

It is best to plan your actual printing to be done in the
middle of a sunny day, when the sun is directly overhead. If the sun is not so bright or not overhead, you
may get shadows and distortion of the design.

Don't limit yourself to only using the "best" artwork.
Sometimes those random notes and scribbles that were
never meant to be presented can be the most interesting. I chose simple drawings, haiku poems, quickly
scratched childhood notes.

In addition to artwork and notes mentioned above, try
taking a side photo of a favorite toy that has a distinc-
tive, recognizable silhouette. As an example, for fun I
added in a silhouette of some bike parts from one of the
kid's first bikes.

I did multiple prints of images I liked. Some objects are
on as many as three blocks.

With a little guidance, the sewing portion of this project
is perfect to try with a child who is interested in learning. Definitely get them involved in the printing part; it
will feel like magic!

Fabric squares printed with lots of imagery will result in
a square that is an overall lighter blue. Squares printed
with only a little imagery will be a darker shade of blue.
This is because the printed areas are lighter than the
unprinted areas. I wanted a good mix of the darker and
lighter blue squares.

I used a favorite African wax print fabric I had on hand
as a backing for my quilt. I wanted the bright all-over
pattern to be a fun surprise when the quilt was turned
over. Find vibrant African wax prints on eBay or Etsy.
They are often sold in 6-yard lengths (enough for most
average-sized quilt backings). Prewash them before using to remove any excess wax from the printing process.

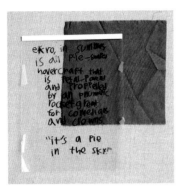

a.

PREPARE ARTWORK FOR PRINTING

1. If using artwork, text, or photographs, scan each piece into your computer in black and white. Most scanners allow you to bump up the contrast, which helps get a clearer image. Play around with the settings in order to get the best image, but you can also fill in any areas that do not print well with a black permanent marker if necessary. If you are using 3-dimensional objects, you may need to first take a picture of it, print it out, then scan the printout to create your image. Print each of these images out on a sheet of transparency film, following the package instructions (see a).

MAKE THE CYANOTYPE PRINTS

Note: There is no need to prewash this fabric.

2. Follow the package instructions for working with the cyanotype fabric. Lay the transparency image or object for your print on top of the fabric square and set it in the direct sun. (Tip: I found it helpful to put the fabric square on a hardcover book, then tape the transparency on the book, over the square, and take it all outside to print.) Test a square before printing all the squares. Remember, the sun should be directly overhead as much as possible, so you don't get shadows on your print.

3. Once the printing is complete, wash and press the squares according to the package instructions.

LAY OUT THE DESIGN

4. On a design wall or cleared surface, lay out the design, in 10 rows of 8 squares each (see b). Move the squares around to your liking, and try having the images face different directions—they don't all have to be oriented the same way. Once the layout feels right, snap a picture of it to refer to later.

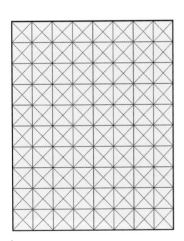

b.

CONSTRUCT THE QUILT TOP

5. Sew the quilt top together in rows, starting from the top left and going across. Press each row's seam allowances going in the opposite direction so the seams will nest and line up when the rows are sewn together.

6. Pin and sew the rows together, starting from the top. I usually add a pin where each of the seams meet to line everything up. Continue until all 10 rows are sewn. Press all the seam allowances to one consistent side.

FINISH THE QUILT

Refer to Quilting 101 (page 145) for more information on each of these steps.

7. Piece fabric together, if needed, to make the quilt backing, which should measure at least 4 inches larger than the finished top's length and width.

Layer the quilt backing, batting, and quilt top to create a quilt sandwich of all 3 layers. Pin baste the layers together.

8. Quilt the layers. I used a walking foot fitted on my sewing machine, and quilted simple diagonal lines through every square, going in both directions (see b) in deep blue coordinating thread, to create a diamond pattern across the quilt. Mark guidelines using a ruler and a marking pen or painter's blue tape.

9. When you are finished quilting, square up the edges of the quilt to be 64 × 80 inches or your desired size.

10. Prepare the binding and bind the quilt following the instructions on page 154.

11. Label your quilt following the instructions on page 156.

20

Cameo

Crazy quilts can be, sometimes, a bit crazy. But they are always infinitely interesting! Vintage ones can often incorporate bits of clothing and very special fabrics from any and everywhere, and they are usually finished off with embellishments like buttons, elaborate hand embroidery, and beads. My interpretation of a crazy quilt is a little less labor-intensive but just as personal. I made silhouettes of my family by taking a picture of each of us using the camera on my phone, then manipulated the images on my computer using Adobe Photoshop. I printed the final images on custom quilting weight fabric from Spoonflower (see Resources). You can simplify this process however you like (see suggestions following).

The method used for piecing smaller pieces of fabric around the center images in this quilt is similar to creating the colorful centers of *Frock* (page 61), but no foundation fabric is needed this time. This project even plays a little with the trapunto effect used in *Taupe* (page 85), which is done underneath the silhouette images to add more dimension and emphasis to them.

This project is an ideal way to use up tiny scraps of favorite fabrics, or do as I did and let each person pick a favorite color for his or her block.

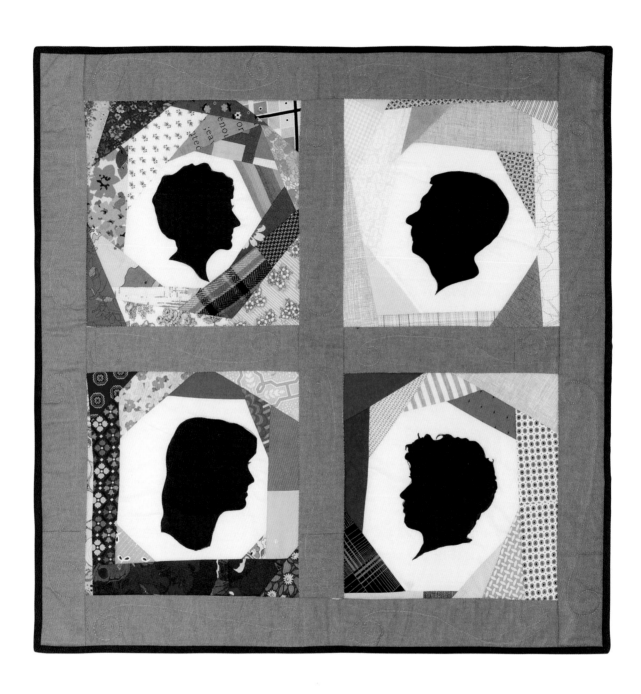

Finished Quilt Size:
25 × 25 inches, for a wall hanging

Finished Block Size:
9½ × 9½ inches

Techniques: Improvisational piecing, creating custom fabric, adding sashing around blocks, creating a hanging sleeve, free motion quilting, trapunto

Fabrics

For the Feature Fabric: Four 7-inch squares of quilting weight cotton fabric with silhouette images for the block centers

For the Top: Assorted fabric scraps of various sizes in favorite colors and patterns; ½ yard 44-inch-wide solid quilting cotton for framing the blocks (I used Robert Kaufman Carolina Chambray in Brown.)

For the Backing: ¾ yard 44-inch-wide quilting cotton fabric. Backing should be least 4 inches larger than your quilt top's total length and width.

For the Binding: ¼ yard 44-inch-wide solid quilting cotton in a coordinating color

Feature Fabric Suggestion: See the notes below for creating the silhouette fabric.

Other Materials

A silhouette photo of each person (or pet) you want to include

Computer, design software like Adobe Photoshop, Illustrator, and an online photo site that will allow you to create silhouette images of your photos or other materials to create your silhouette (see Resources)

Low-Loft Cotton Batting: Package craft-sized batting cut to size. Batting should be least 4 inches larger than your quilt top's total length and width.

High-Loft Batting: ¼ yard for trapunto details (I used Quilter's Dream Puff.)

My Color and Design Notes

I created my silhouette images by loading pictures taken of each of us onto my computer. I opened each image

in Adobe Illustrator and painted our faces black and replaced the background with solid white. I then uploaded the silhouette images to Spoonflower (see Resources) and had them printed onto quilting weight cotton.

If my approach is beyond your tools or abilities, you can make your silhouettes in other ways: use free online tools (see Resources) that allow you to create different types of images from photographs; scan a photo or other image into your computer and print it directly onto printable fabric sheets that can go through your home printer, available at craft stores; use fabric markers or paint to draw silhouettes directly onto your fabric; cut a silhouette from fabric and appliqué it on your fabric block; use a Frixion or water-soluble pen to trace the outline of your silhouette at a sunny window and then embroider or free motion quilt along the lines directly on the fabric blocks.

The silhouettes in my quilt are surrounded by small scraps of fabric. I have more than enough fabric scraps to last the rest of my life, and I group the smallest bits in bins by color in my studio. When I was making this piece, I asked each person to pick his or her favorite color/scrap bin. All the scraps that surround an individual's silhouette were pulled from that bin. I allowed about an inch or so of room between where the silhouette image ends, and where I began sewing the scraps around it. This is simply a guide; moving the scraps a little closer to the silhouette will allow you to fit more on, and vice versa.

As more and more fabrics are added around the block, some of the beginning scraps may get smaller and all but disappear. I actually consider it a happy surprise when all that's visible of a fabric is a tiny little piece that would be nearly impossible to sew on any other way.

It was really helpful to keep my iron set up near my sewing machine for this project. Each new fabric addition will need to be pressed open before adding the next piece.

Before sewing each new scrap fabric down, lay it in place, right side up, on the block, to see that it is a good fit for size and coverage. Next, without repositioning the fabric, just flip the fabric wrong side up in place before sewing.

I played with the idea of having my silhouettes framed like a picture by using a brown chambray fabric to create framing strips around each of the blocks.

CREATE SILHOUETTE IMAGES

1. Using your preferred method, create your silhouette images. The art should be about the same size and centered on fabric blocks. I used 7-inch feature fabric blocks with silhouette images roughly 5 x 5 inches. This allowed me a generous inch or so of space between the image and where I began adding the fabric scraps around the silhouette.

ADD CRAZY PIECING AROUND THE SILHOUETTE

a.

b.

2. Add fabric scraps around each silhouette working in a clockwise direction. You will have to go around the square, adding fabric, as many times as needed to end up with a square that measures at least 10 inches. To sew a piece of fabric, lay the scrap across 1 edge of the silhouette fabric square, starting at 1 o'clock (see a, b). Position the scrap 1 inch or so away from the edge of the silhouette, so that there is just a little room between them. Flip the scrap over in place, so that right sides are facing each other. Stitch it onto the feature fabric, pressing the seam allowance away from the silhouette, and trim any excess scrap fabric seam allowance beyond ¼ inch (don't trim the silhouette fabric yet). Move around the square, adding a new scrap overlapping the edge of the previous one, sew down, trim any extra scrap seam allowance, and press. Continue adding scraps, periodically checking the overall size of the block. You may need to add more scraps to one side of the block to keep the silhouette centered, which is the goal. The scraps should not be a uniform size. Add more where you need to in order to create the look you want in the block.

3. Continue sewing to make the block slightly bigger than you need. Measure and trim it down to 10 × 10 inches.

4. Make a total of 4 blocks (or the amount desired).

CUT AND SEW THE FRAMING STRIPS

5. From the ½ yard of solid quilting cotton, cut the following strips, selvedge to selvedge:

Two strips measuring 2½ × 25 inches wide

Three strips measuring 2½ × 21 inches wide

Two strips measuring 2½ × 10 inches wide

6. Refer to the illustration (see c), and begin laying out the silhouette blocks in a grid of 2 by 2. Position and sew a 2½ × 10-inch framing strip between the 2 horizontal pairs of silhouettes; press the seam allowances toward the strip. Position and sew a 2½ × 21-inch framing strip above the top pair, in the middle between the pairs, and at the bottom of the lower pair; press the seam allowances toward the framing strips. (Tip: Use pins on these longer strip seams.) Line up the framing strip and the piece you will sew it to, wrong sides together, place a pin on each end and one in the center.

7. Last, sew one 2½ × 25-inch framing strip to each of the sides and press the seam allowance toward the framing strip.

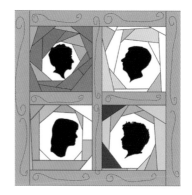

c.

CREATE THE TRAPUNTO DETAILS

8. I added a trapunto layer under each of the silhouettes and outline stitched around each image with matching thread. To do this, cut a piece of high-loft batting slightly larger than the silhouette and place it directly under the image, adding a few pins to secure it in place. Set your sewing machine up for free motion stitching (refer to Quilting 101, page 145), and stitch around the silhouette in coordinating thread, just as if you were free motion quilting. Once done, turn the work over and carefully trim away the extra batting that extends beyond the stitching (do this very carefully, don't cut into the quilt top). Do this for each silhouette.

FINISH THE QUILT

Refer to Quilting 101 (page 145) for more information on each of these steps.

9. Piece fabric together, if needed, to make a quilt backing at least 4 inches larger than the finished top. Layer the quilt backing, batting, and quilt top to create a quilt sandwich of all 3 layers. Pin baste the layers together.

10. Quilt the layers. With the black thread and the free motion foot still set up on my sewing machine, I outlined the silhouettes again to secure them to the batting layer. From there, I switched to a thread matching the framing strips and did a simple swirly design on each of them, reminiscent of the scrollwork you might find on a wooden picture frame (see c). Mark quilting lines using a Frixion or water-soluble marking pen to guide you as you stitch.

11. When finished quilting, square up the edges of the quilt to be 25 × 25 inches or your desired size.

12. Prepare the binding and bind the quilt using the instructions on page 154.

13. Label your quilt following the instructions on page 156.

14. Make a hanging sleeve following the instructions on page 157.

21

Sensory

I was inspired to create this quilt for the aging, loved ones in my life who are perhaps no longer able to live in their homes among the favorite personal belongings and memories they have accumulated over a lifetime. But even if they are still at home, this quilt can be created from things that evoke joy and comfort. A security blanket in every sense of the word.

My friend Ahna Holder made a quilt for her grandmother to spark conversation and trigger memories between them. We ran into each other in a fabric store, years ago, while she was picking fabrics for what would become the inspiration quilt. In Ahna's words:

> My grandma Doris is ninety-four years old. She and my grandpa got married and started their family at eighteen, so I was very fortunate to have them both around for almost all of my life. After my grandpa passed away, I would talk to my grandma about everything that I could remember, from her stories about growing up, things that she and my grandpa did together, to pretty much anything I could think of. We'd look through photo albums, and talk. But soon, I noticed that she wasn't really seeing the pictures and wasn't contributing as much to the conversations. I was having to work harder at keeping her interest. She tended to fidget with things, especially her large rings that she wore. And if someone removed them, and forgot to put them back on, she'd ask repeatedly where they were. I got the idea for my grandma's quilt because I needed some more things to talk about! I wanted the quilt to relate to her stories and to have things she could touch and pick at if she wanted to; it needed to be big so she could see it and colorful, very colorful.

This quilt celebrates the person it is made for, and is made unique to their stories and memories. I imagined a version of a *Sensory* as I would have made it for my grandmother who passed away years ago. She taught me many of the handcrafts that are an important part of my life today. Her flowers were something she took great pride in. With this quilt, we could sit together and talk about all the flowers that made up the quilt and smile together over their lovely colors and patterns.

Making a sensory quilt for a loved one is truly a labor of love. Consider what makes that person's heart sing, celebrate what makes them who they are and what they mean to you.

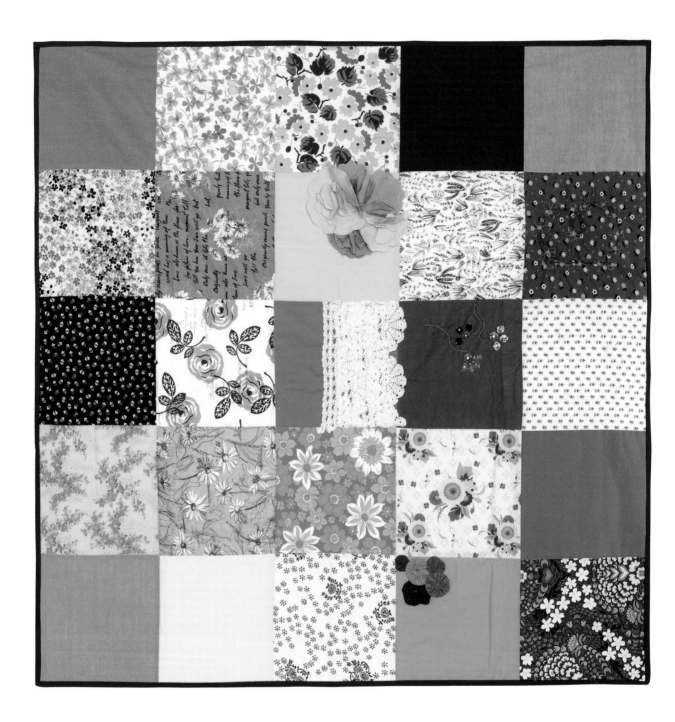

Finished Quilt Size:
42½ × 42½ inches,
for a lap-sized quilt

Finished Block Size:
8½ × 8½ inches

Techniques: Adding surface
texture, simple square patchwork,
walking foot quilting in the ditch

Fabrics

For the Feature Fabric: Twenty-five 9-inch squares

For the Backing: 2 yards 44-inch-wide quilting cotton
fabric. Backing should be least 4 inches larger than
your quilt top's total length and width.

For the Binding: ⅓ yard 44-inch-wide solid quilting
cotton

Feature Fabric Suggestion: In addition to cotton prints,
I added corduroy fabrics to provide texture. Think of
fabrics that will please the quilt's recipient: a favorite
flannel shirt, a print from their curtains, anything that
will bring a smile to their face. Bright, vivid colors may
delight someone whose eyesight may not be as sharp as
it once was.

Other Materials

Special items that can be sewn on the quilt surface:
Consider pockets, lace, favorite doilies, handkerchiefs,
buttons, beads, and other types of things special to the
recipient.

Template for fabric flowers, optional

Low-Loft Cotton Batting: 1 package crib-sized batting
cut to size. Batting should be least 4 inches larger than
your quilt top's total length and width.

Color and Design Notes

I suggest using a cotton flannel backing fabric for this
project. If used as a lap quilt, the flannel is not only cozy
and warm, but it will less likely slip off the person's lap.

It is best if everything used to adorn the quilt (trims,
beads, etc.) is secured well to the quilt and machine
washable. This will not always be possible, but it should
be the goal. For my quilt, I made 6 fabric flowers in various colors and sizes out of solid green quilting cotton
and stitched them onto 1 green square. They are secure
at their base, but they flutter and are fun to fidget with. I
created a patch pocket in a clover printed fabric, which
I stitched onto a similar clover print square. I created
a small lavender sachet sewn from two 3-inch-square
pieces of muslin. I also used part of a vintage doily to
add some contrast embroider details.

On a darker blue square, I sewed Swarovski crystals in
a floral pattern. These are some of my favorite embellishments and make anything I sew them to feel extra
fancy and pretty. (This is similar to the way I embellished *Frock*, page 61.)

On the green floral patterned square, I free motion
stitched a layer of trapunto batting underneath a few
of the flowers just to add dimension (similar to *Taupe*,
page 85). I printed out a large letter monogram from
my computer, traced it onto a green floral square, and
free motion stitched around it (similar to the center
motif of *Whole Cloth*, page 29). I also made several
fabric yo-yos and sewed them onto a light blue square.
All of these adornments add surface interest and can be
touched and fidgeted with.

Keep in mind that the squares at the center area of the
quilt are what people will see first when they place the
quilt in their laps. This is the area to add special touches
that will get attention and be noticed from day to day.

PREPARE THE FABRIC

1. Refer to the section Preparing Vintage and Secondhand Fabric on page 150 for information on preparing your fabric.

CUT THE SQUARES

2. Cut 9-inch squares from the fabrics. You will need a total of 25.

LAY OUT THE DESIGN

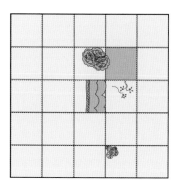

a.

3. On a design wall or cleared surface, lay out the design, in 5 rows of 5 squares each (see a), moving squares around to create nice visual movement in the design. If you are using directional prints, have some oriented in different directions, not all facing the same way. Once the layout feels right, snap a picture of it to refer to later.

CONSTRUCT THE QUILT TOP

4. Sew the quilt top together in rows, starting from the top left and going across. Press each row's seam allowances in the opposite direction so the seams will nest and line up when the rows are sewn together.

5. Pin and sew the rows together, starting from the top. Press all the seam allowances to one side.

ADD THE EMBELLISHMENTS

6. To make fabric flowers, print the template out at full size (page 164) and cut it out. On your chosen flower fabric, trace the large template 2 times, and the smaller template 4 times. Cut the flowers out, and cut into each flower as indicated on the template (no need to finish the raw edges). You will attach each flower segment by stitching through the center of it; do not stitch down the edges of the petals. Begin by layering both large flower shapes directly over each other, rotating the top shape 90 degrees to vary the placement of the petals. Secure them directly onto the quilt surface with several hand stitches through the centers. To create layers of floral petals, fold 1 smaller fabric shape in half and secure it to the center area of the large flower shapes with hand stitches, catching and stitching the fold down. Add each new smaller flower shape the same way, but rotate it 90 degrees and layer over the previous shape.

7. To make a patch pocket, cut a 4 × 8-inch piece of fabric and fold it in half lengthwise, right sides together; press. Stitch around the perimeter of the square, using a ¼-inch seam allowance, and leaving a 1½-inch opening along one side for turning. Clip the corners, turn the pocket right side out, and press. Place the square on the quilt top. Pin it in place and stitch it to quilt along the sides and bottom, capturing and closing the turning opening as you sew.

8. To add a doily detail, cut the doily into strips, following the design of the piece (my strips were scalloped along the edges). Sew the 4 strips of the doily by sewing across the cut edge onto the front of 1 square using coordinating thread. Add some embroidery details by hand stitching a few stitches through the pattern of the doily using a contrast color. This detail looks pretty and functions to help hold the strips down. (I used a bright green embroidery floss.)

9. Continue adding embellishments as you like (see further suggestions above).

FINISH THE QUILT

Refer to Quilting 101 (page 145) for more information on each of these steps.

10. Piece fabric together, if needed, to make the quilt backing, which should measure at least 4 inches larger than the finished top's length and width. Layer the quilt backing, batting, and quilt top to create a quilt sandwich of all 3 layers. Pin baste the layers together.

11. Quilt the layers. I kept the quilting simple on this project, and used the walking foot fitted on my sewing machine to stitch in the ditch along all the seams of the patchwork squares, using a coordinating thread. This is plenty of quilting for this piece, and I didn't stitch over any of the embellishments.

12. When you are finished quilting, square up the edges of the quilt to be 42½ × 42½ inches or your desired size.

13. Prepare the binding and bind the quilt following the instructions on page 154.

14. Label your quilt following the instructions on page 156.

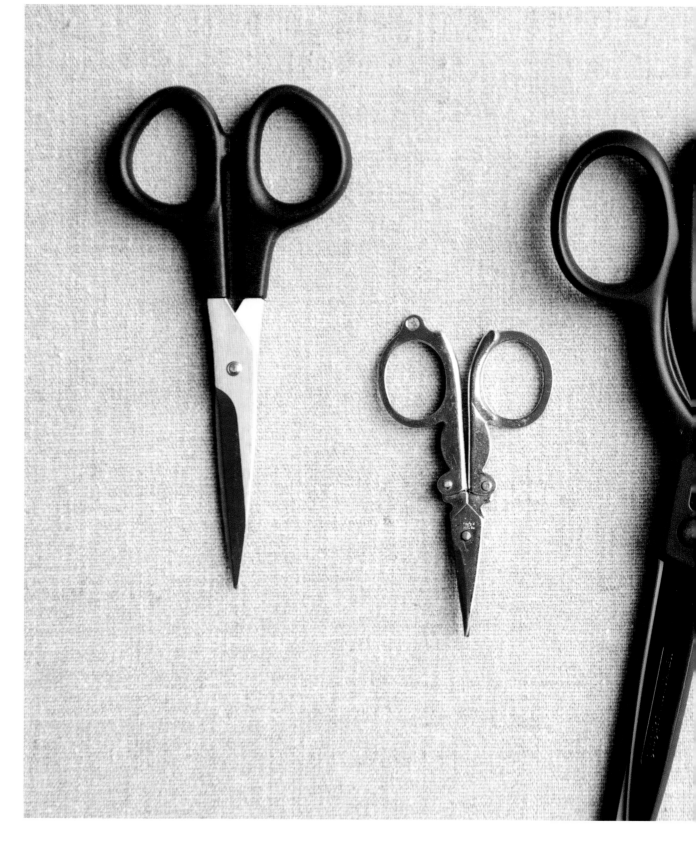

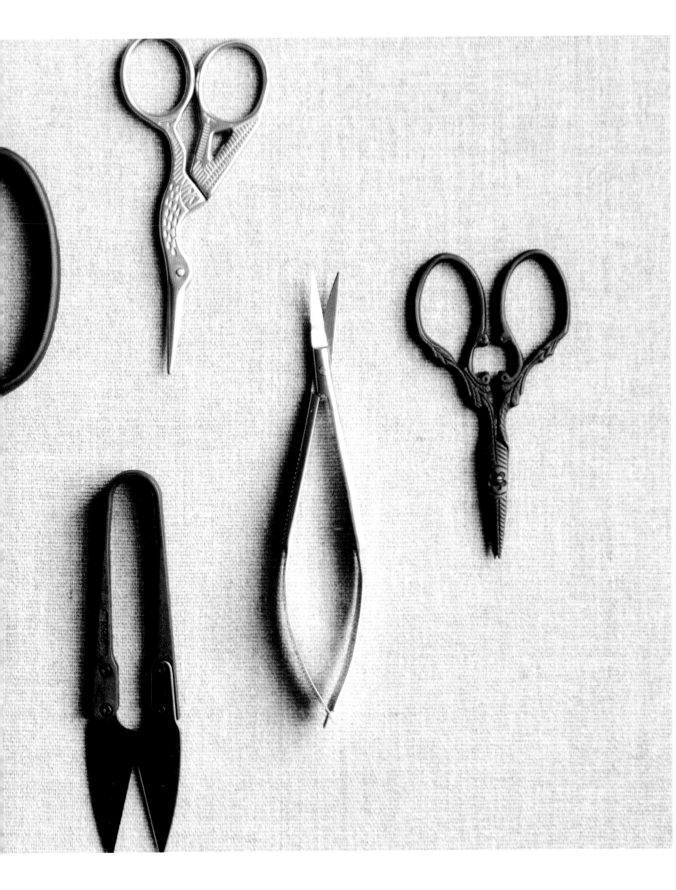

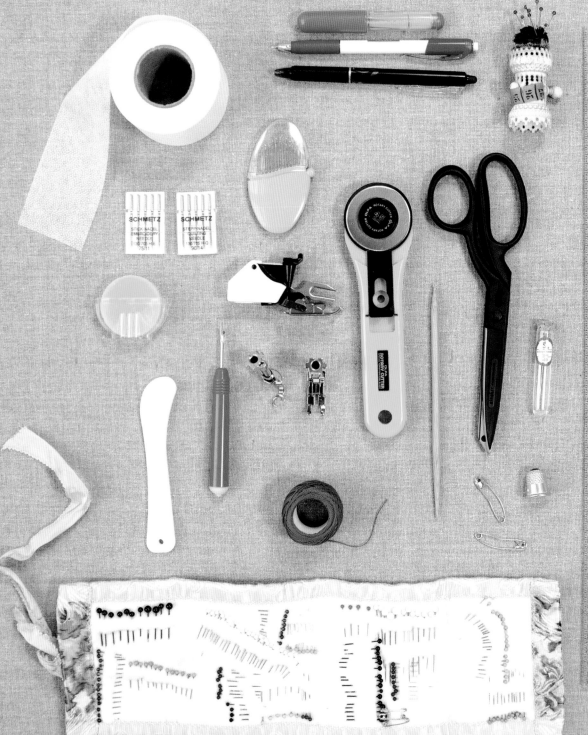

Quilting 101

This section offers some guidelines for making the projects in this book. The project instructions will refer you to specific techniques here as needed, but it's also a good idea to review these notes before getting started.

Quilter's Tool Kit

There are countless methods and techniques for making a quilt, but they all start with some basic tools. You will pull supplies from this tool kit for each of the projects in this book.

I recommend supplies and tools that are comfortable to hold and pretty whenever possible; they are just more enjoyable to use. The following list contains the ones I depend on for my quilt making and recommend to others. Most of these are readily available at most fabric and craft stores.

We are all busy, and sometimes patchwork designing, cutting, or sewing can happen in fits and starts. Take a few minutes to gather these items together and you'll be ready anytime the inspiration strikes.

SCISSORS—Invest in a good quality pair that feels comfortable in your hand. Label them as fabric only (I like to tie a piece of fabric on the handle) and designate them off-limits from everyone else. Or better yet, hide them. Also helpful is a pair used only for paper (for cutting out templates). Small, sharp thread snips and embroidery scissors are good to have when hand sewing or trimming loose thread tails. Pinking shears are useful to recut fabric edges of delicate fabrics to inhibit fraying.

SEAM RIPPER—We all need at least one, so make it a cute one that is comfortable to hold and use.

ROTARY CUTTER AND REPLACEMENT BLADES—I have used the same 45 mm rotary cutter from Olfa for ten years. I replace the blade regularly because I tend to cut through several layers of fabric at a time, which dulls the blade quickly. Always exercise care when using a rotary cutter, and close the blade when it's not in use.

QUILTER'S CLEAR RULERS—These rulers are used in combination with a rotary cutter. I most often use Omnigrid acrylic rulers, which have clearly marked lines in ⅛-inch increments. You need at least one; 3 × 18 inch is a good size to start with. Some of the other sizes I like are 3½ × 24-inch, 6 × 12-inch, and 12½-inch square. Lay these rulers over the fabric to allow you to line up the exact cutting edge; make a cut by running the rotary cutter along the edge (always away from you) to make a clean, straight cut.

SELF-HEALING CUTTING MAT—Rotary cutting must always be done on one of these cutting mats. A good one to start with is the Olfa 18 × 24 inches.

PINS AND PINCUSHIONS—I suggest you have a few types of pins on hand to accommodate different types of fabrics. For general quilt making, I prefer Clover flower head pins. They are long, sharp, strong, and easy to grab and remove as I sew. (It only takes one pin to cause damage to you or your machine, so do not make a habit of sewing over them.) I also recommend a couple of pincushions. I have a magnetic one, which quickly grabs a stack of pins that have fallen on the floor or cutting table, and a prettier, woolen one filled with my hand-sewing needles.

SEWING MACHINE—A basic sewing machine with the ability to make a steady, straight stitch is all you need for the projects in this book. It is helpful if you have the ability to drop or cover the feed dogs that guide the fabric under the presser foot, allowing you to do free motion quilting. Check your manual. Make sure it's in good working order, cleaning out lint often and oiling it regularly. Give your sewing machine a name. *It is just that special.*

SEWING MACHINE NEEDLES—For basic patchwork, I use Schmetz 80/12 needle, but I also have a variety of needle sizes on hand for sewing through delicate, vintage fabrics, as well as thick fabrics like denim. Replace the sewing needle often; I recommend a fresh needle at the start of every project, but as a general guideline, change the needle after every six hours of sewing.

PATCHWORK FOOT, WALKING FOOT, AND FREE MOTION FOOT— Having this assortment of presser feet for your sewing machine provides you with lots of flexibility when sewing quilts. Use a patchwork foot to line up the fabric's edge with the edge of the foot and achieve a consistent ¼-inch seam allowance, which is the standard for quilt making. A walking foot has feed dogs that work with the feed dogs under the presser foot to guide multiple fabric layers through the machine evenly. A free motion foot, also called a darning foot, allows you to move the quilt freely under the presser foot. If you drop or cover the feed dogs below the presser foot, this foot allows you to create all sorts of free motion quilting stitches on your quilt. (Read more about this in the section on Quilting the Layers, page 152.) If your machine does not come with these feet, do a little research. They can usually be bought separately and are worth having if you plan to sew quilts regularly.

THREAD—I use Aurifil Mako 50 weight cotton thread for my patchwork sewing, free motion quilting, and hand sewing. I keep cones of a light, medium, and dark shade on hand for general patchwork sewing and buy specific colors to use for free motion quilting. This thread is thin, strong, high quality, and universal, suitable for all kinds of fabrics. I do not recommend polyester or poly-wrapped thread, which can actually begin to cut into cotton fabrics as the quilt ages.

IRON AND IRONING BOARD—I use a hot iron with steam for general patchwork but adjust it for delicate fabrics. Keep it close to the sewing machine, as there tends to be a lot of back and forth between it and the machine when sewing patchwork.

SMOOTHING SPRAY—I do not use spray starch on my quilts when ironing; the cornstarch in it can attract bugs if the quilt is stored. I prefer to use a flattening spray like Flatter. It works to remove wrinkles and smooth the fabric as it is ironed. A bonus is it leaves your sewing space smelling wonderful!

PRESS CLOTH—For me this is just a scrap piece of clean muslin kept at the ironing board. I use it over delicate fabrics when I'm ironing and when I'm fusing interfacing.

DESIGN WALL—Individual pieces of a patchwork design need to be laid out and considered together before being sewn. This can absolutely be done on a cleared floor or table, but I find putting the components up on a vertical wall, where I can stand back and get a little distance from the design, is best. You can make a portable design wall by taping a white or cream flannel sheet around a large piece of foam core board or a door, or simply tack a flannel sheet up on a wall. Cotton quilting fabrics naturally "stick" to the flannel (think preschool flannel storyboards), allowing you to lay out the entire design before you begin sewing.

REDUCING GLASS—This may sound mysterious, but it's not. I use a door peephole I purchased from the hardware store. You could also use the wrong side of a magnifying glass. Looking through these allows you to view your entire quilt on the design wall without having to stand a mile away. It can also help you see that you have a good distribution of color across the quilt top, determine if the design is clearly visible, and give you a sense of your quilt from a distance. If you are using the color value of your fabrics to define your design, a reducing glass is essential for seeing that the pattern is discernable and that value shifts in the design make sense.

SMARTPHONE OR DIGITAL CAMERA—Take a picture of your full layout to refer to later, before taking things off the design wall to sew them. Trust me.

MARKING PENS—There are all kinds of marking pens for quilters. My suggestion is to try a variety and decide what you like best. Most of the projects in this book recommend a Frixion pen (my favorite, I use blue or black) or a water-soluble fabric marker. Marks made with the Frixion will disappear with the heat of an iron. I have been told that the marks made with these pens can come back when the quilt is exposed to cold temperatures, but I have never had that happen. A toss around in the dryer or a warm iron would make the marks vanish again, but it is always good to test any marking pencil or pen on your fabric first to be sure the marks will disappear. These pens can be used to mark quilting lines, trace around appliqué templates, and mark stitching lines when needed.

HERA MARKER—This plastic tool leaves a visible crease line on the fabric and is good for marking long quilting lines. Just line up the edge of an acrylic ruler where you wish to mark, and run the hera marker alongside the edge of it a couple of times to create a creased line. Some prefer these to marking pens. If you are unsure about how your fabric will take a marking pen, use a hera marker instead.

SEWING STILETTO—Essentially, this tool is a pointy stick. I use a sewing stiletto often to hold and guide my patchwork under the sewing machine's presser foot, in place of a pin. It keeps my fingers from wandering too close to the needle.

HAND-SEWING NEEDLES AND A THIMBLE—Have a variety pack of good-quality needles on hand to ensure you have the type you need for your project. I prefer John James needles. I personally have never been able to use a traditional metal thimble when I hand quilt, but I recently starting trying out a leather version and find it very comfortable. I have also been known to cover my fingertip with a bandage instead.

QUILTER'S SAFETY PINS—These pins are curved and designed to be used to pin baste quilt layers together. Pinned through all three layers of the quilt sandwich to baste the layers together, they will help keep your layers together smoothly if done well, an important step before quilting your quilt. In my experience, quilter's pins can at times leave large holes in the fabric, which I don't like. I have developed an alternative method of basting the layers using straight pins, which you can find on my blog (www.wisecrafthandmade.com).

TEMPORARY BASTING SPRAY ADHESIVE—A basting spray is helpful for certain kinds of fabrics and used to hold quilt layers together smoothly instead of pin basting. I recommend 505 Spray and Fix. Use it according to the package instructions in a well-ventilated area.

PAINTER'S BLUE TAPE—This low-tack tape, available at hardware stores, is helpful for laying out quilt backing smoothly, as well as for marking long straight quilting lines when hand or machine quilting.

FRAY BLOCKER—Brush this liquid on the raw edges of delicate fabrics to prevent fraying. I keep a small bottle nearby and use a tiny bit along the raw edges whenever I am cutting into a finicky fabric. My favorite type is Fray Block with Precise Applicator Brush by June Tailor.

FUSIBLE BATTING TAPE—I don't like to waste scraps of batting, and I use this iron-on tape to join smaller pieces together for bigger projects. I like Dritz 1½-inch-wide Iron-On Fusible Batting Tape. Join a couple of larger pieces together by straightening the two edges you want to join, align them side by side (not overlapping), and iron a strip of this tape to cover the join line on the front and back of the batting seam. Works like a charm.

WATER-SOLUBLE APPLIQUÉ GLUE—I use this glue instead of pins to hold down a fabric motif I plan to appliqué onto a base fabric. I like Roxanne's Glue Baste It liquid and Sewline water-soluble fabric glue pen. Both create a strong, temporary hold and will wash out of your fabric.

QUILTING HOOP—Use a hoop when you have hand quilting to do. It looks similar to an embroidery hoop but is larger and used to secure the layers of a quilt before hand quilting. I have never been very skilled at using it, but I still try because it is very helpful at keeping stitching tension consistent and the fabric taut and even.

QUILTING GLOVES—These gloves are ideal when you are quilting on your home sewing machine. They have a texture to them that allows you to grip and move the bulky, heavy quilt layers around without slipping or pulling.

BINDING CLIPS—These clips are useful when hand sewing the binding to the back of the quilt. Fold the binding over the quilt's edge ahead of where you are sewing and clip to hold everything in place. You can also use straight pins or clothespins.

Building Your Fabric Collection

Collections of textiles for quilt making can be found everywhere, possibly even beginning in your own closet. Well-made clothing from beautiful fabrics can easily be reused in quilt form once they become stained or deemed out of style. Start conversations with loved ones and they may soon be pulling collections of keepsake fabrics out of storage. Anything can work: fabrics collected by a great aunt, a grandmother's tatted lace doilies, or a collection of linens used for years of family dinners. These are all worthy of being out and enjoyed in our everyday lives. They are a part of who we are and where we came from. There is so much joy to using them and having them live with us in our own home.

Other times we can create our own collections of textiles. If your grandmother lived in colorful Marimekko dresses but there were none to be saved, add a search for these fabrics to your list of eBay or local thrift stores queries. Even one small piece of fabric with special meaning can be the focus of an entire quilt. One idea is to use it as a special spirit cloth quilt project as I did in *Spirit* (page 69). Fabric and textile collections are all around us. Looking for them and acquiring them is half the fun.

Preparing Vintage and Secondhand Fabric

I prewash all secondhand and vintage fabric as soon as I bring it home for several reasons. Often the haphazard storage conditions of older fabrics—long-term folds that weaken the fiber's edges, sun damage, humidity or lack of—can leave them looking and smelling musty and dingy. Cleaning can also determine if a fabric is simply too weak or damaged, from factors such as dry rot, to be used in a quilt. It is always better to find these things out early, before planning and beginning a project. Thoroughly cleaned and pressed is the best way to store old fabric.

I have been a complete textile science geek since studying textile science in college. With experience over the years, I have refined how I clean all the thrifted and vintage fabrics I bring home. Most of these fabrics are stronger than you think and only need a little bit of extra TLC in the beginning to ensure success. My overall general rule is to wash the fabrics as the final quilt will be washed. If the quilt will be adored, used regularly, and perhaps even dragged around by its owner, I will prewash the fabrics knowing the finished quilt will need machine washing at regular intervals. Do I plan to frame the piece and hang it on a wall? Perhaps the fabrics will only need a delicate prewash to remove discoloration or mildew.

The musty smell of old fabric comes from bacteria introduced into the fibers due to factors such as water damage or general storage conditions. I have had great success using a product called BioKleen to remove this (see Resources). I thoroughly spray and saturate the entire textile with this cleaner, allowing the live enzymes to settle in the fibers and do their work for several hours, sometimes even overnight for heavily soiled cloth (exposure time is key for this product to do its work). Next, without rinsing, I wash the fabric in a product called Retro Clean (see Resources). I follow the package instructions, filling the washer (or sink), adding the fabric, and allowing the fabric to soak in the soapy water for one hour up to overnight, depending on the amount of staining. For this step, it is always best to wash larger pieces of yardage, but if you must wash small scraps, keep them together in lingerie bags. If fraying edges are a concern, use pinking shears to trim the ends before washing. Wash deeply colored fabrics separately to test how colorfast the piece is, and keep refilling the sink and rinsing the fabric until the water runs clear. I never use chlorine bleach; it will weaken the fibers as it eats away at the discoloration. Nor I have ever had much success using color safe bleach. Once the fabric is rinsed completely, dry in the sunshine on a sunny day (sun is a natural antibacterial) or on low heat in a dryer.

After these steps, if the fabric is determined in good shape and useable, I press it well and keep it stored away from direct sunlight until I am ready to use it in a sewing project. Once I decide on a quilt project and choose the fabrics, I usually wash the fabrics again, this time all together, to be sure everything is colorfast. I will often throw a color catcher sheet in with the fabrics I prewash in the washing machine, to soak up any small amounts of loose dye that may bleed from the fabrics, just as a little extra assurance. These techniques have worked for me for many years, reviving dull fabric, leaving it clean, bright, fresh, and ready to be used alongside other new and vintage fabrics in my quilts with no problem.

General Patchwork Sewing

Patchwork pieces are always sewn with right sides together, using a ¼-inch seam allowance, unless otherwise noted in the instructions. This seam allowance is much smaller than that used in garment sewing, and it may take getting used to if you are new to quilting. An accurate, consistent ¼-inch seam is important to achieve good results. A patchwork foot attached to your sewing machine makes this easy—just line the edge of the fabric up with the edge of the presser foot. If your machine doesn't come with a patchwork foot, it can usually be bought separately. You can also measure ¼ inch from your needle and mark it with a strip of tape on the bed of your machine.

There is no need to backstitch at the beginning and end of a stitching line unless specified in the instructions. All patchwork stitch lines get crossed with other stitching lines, securing everything just fine.

Use the normal stitch length on your sewing machine. If your machine has a needle down function, use it. For good sewing performance, it is helpful to change the sewing needle after every six hours of sewing. Clean and oil the bobbin case with every bobbin reload. I like to use a pipe cleaner instead of the brush that comes with my sewing machine to clean this area. Lint seems to cling to it better. By keeping your machine clean, you will be rewarded with nice, even tension and smooth stitches.

Making the Quilt Back

Your quilt will need a fabric backing, and I recommend making it at least 4 inches larger than the quilt top's total length and width, which will give you an extra 2 inches of backing extending beyond the quilt top on each side, once the quilt top is centered over it. This will allow for any shifting of the layers that can occur during the quilting process. Don't try to use a backing that measures the same size as the quilt top. It just doesn't work well. Ask me how I know.

Backings can be as intricately pieced or as simple as you are inspired to make them. I tend to go with simply pieced backings, often using a bedsheet cut to size (a flannel one is nice and cozy) or a large beautiful print that complements the colors on the front of the quilt. If I come across a pretty quilting cotton, I will buy at least 3 or 4 yards to use it as a backing for a future quilt. It is easy to piece lengths of it together to achieve the size I need. A printed fabric helps camouflage the quilting stitches on the back (it also hides the mistakes). I recommend pressing the seam allowances open to reduce bulk at the seams. I also often purchase extra-wide (108 inches) quilting fabric made specifically for backings, eliminating any need for piecing. I do not use vintage or secondhand fabric for my quilt backings, mainly because I usually don't have enough of any one fabric and prefer not to piece quilt backs.

Batting

There are all types of quilt battings available, and I've tried most of them. Most of the quilts I make are meant to be used and washed regularly, so I recommend low-loft Quilters Regal Dream Cotton batting in a natural or white color. It allows quilting stitches up to 8 inches apart (less work for us!), resists creasing when the quilt is folded, holds up beautifully over time, and has minimal shrinkage.

Whatever type of batting you buy, read the packaging information carefully to be sure it fits the needs of your quilt. There is no need to prewash or iron the batting before using it in the quilt; just be sure it is flat and smooth between the layers. As with the backing, I recommend making it at least 4 inches larger than the quilt top's total length and width, which will give you an extra 2 inches extending beyond the quilt top on each side, once the quilt top is centered over it.

Creating the Quilt Sandwich

Unless noted otherwise, the quilts in this book are made with a top layer of patchwork, a middle layer of batting or wadding, and a backing layer. These three layers together are what is referred to as the quilt sandwich, and they must be basted together before the quilting process, which will permanently hold them together. It is worth taking the time to do a thorough job of layering to avoid puckers. I usually baste using pins, and I have created a method of basting on a tabletop that works well for me, which you can find on my blog (www.wisecrafthandmade.com). Quilter's safety pins, which are bent in the middle, work well for the basting process, but regular safety pins work too. Basting sprays are also available to baste your quilt sandwich.

Create your quilt sandwich on your worktable or cleared floor. Start by laying out the pressed backing layer, wrong side up. Tape it down to the surface on all four sides with painter's blue tape to ensure it is flat. Center the batting layer over the backing, smoothing it into place. Last, lay the quilt top over the batting, right side up. Baste all three layers together using your preferred method, working from the center and moving out, smoothing as you go. If you are using pins, place them every 4 to 6 inches (I use my fist as a general guide). Once the layers are together, remove the painter's tape.

Quilting the Layers

Securing all three layers together with some sort of decorative or functional stitches is the actual quilting process. There are several ways to do this. In fact, whole books are written on the subject. Here are brief descriptions of the different methods I used in the projects in this book.

TYING

If a quilt has thick layers, or if I think it would add to the overall design, I will often tie the quilt layers together using wool yarn. I mark a grid of dots across the top of the quilt. At each of these dots, I will stitch a length of yarn through all three layers and tie it in a square knot, usually on the front of the quilt (although sometimes it looks nice to tie it on the back).

HAND QUILTING

This is something you may enjoy if you like to embroider. Traditional hand quilting uses a thread made specifically for quilting, and it is done with very tiny stitches. The type of hand quilting I prefer uses larger stitches, usually done in a contrasting color of Perle cotton size 8 thread. Hand quilt around areas of the quilt that you want to emphasize or that need a little extra something. A quilt that is entirely hand quilted tends to be lighter and have more drape than one with dense machine quilting. I use hand quilting in combination with free motion quilting on *Spirit* (page 69).

WALKING FOOT QUILTING

I will use the walking presser foot on my sewing machine to stitch a series of straight lines across the quilt top. These usually go in a straight grid pattern, or my personal favorite, a diamond pattern, which I mark on the quilt top with a Frixion pen, hera marker, or painter's blue tape.

FREE MOTION QUILTING

Free motion quilting is fast becoming my favorite method of quilting my quilts, and I have used this method for several of the quilts in this book. Attach a free motion embroidery or darning presser foot to your sewing machine. You will also need to either drop the feed dogs that are located under the presser foot (some machines have a button or lever to do this; check your manual) or cover them so that they will not move the fabric. The feed dogs move the fabric in one direction under the pressure foot. You want to be able to move the fabric freely under the presser foot and "draw" with the thread. These simple adjustments allow you to essentially draw with your stitches. It may take a little practice, but getting the hang of it can add a lot of dimension to your quilts. Before beginning to free motion quilt, always let your needle go down into the fabric, then bring it up again (creating one stitch in place). Pull at the top thread, and the bobbin thread will come up to the top as well. Doing this before stitching will prevent a nest of bobbin thread on the back of the quilt as you begin stitching. Also before you begin, take a few teeny tiny stitches in place to hold the stitches. When ready, you will draw with thread, sewing through all the layers. Remember, the feed dogs are no longer moving your fabric under the presser foot, so you will need to keep moving the fabric as you stitch to avoid a buildup of stitches in one spot. When you are finished stitching an area and wish to "break thread," take a few teeny tiny stitches in place to hold the stitches.

I usually draw the general design idea of what I want to free motion quilt directly on the quilt top with a Frixion pen before I start. Keep in mind that free motion can be a very improvisational process, and you may just decide to throw caution to the wind and start stitching without marking. There is no one right way to do it.

PROFESSIONAL LONG ARM QUILTER

Although it can be pricey, this is an option if quilting the layers together is not something you enjoy. Professional quilters will usually charge by the inch for an all-over design, more for a custom design. Consulting with them on your quilt top and creating a unique design together can really add a lot of interest and beauty to your quilt. Keep in mind, it is best to consult with professionals before basting any of the layers together; they will let you know how they prefer this to be done. I consulted with a long arm quilter for quilting *Value* (page 47). We collaborated on how to show off the different areas with quilting stitches, and it was fun to get her input.

Squaring Up the Quilt Layers

Regardless of the quilting method you choose, you will need to square up all four sides of the quilt before the binding step. I have a large square quilt ruler that I use for this step, but any longer clear quilting ruler will do. Measure the length and width at the top, middle, and bottom of the quilt top and average them out to get the final dimensions your quilt should be. Hopefully, squaring up the edges won't require trimming away more than a tiny bit of the quilt top; this process should be more about trimming away the extra batting and backing and creating a straight edge to apply the binding. I start in one corner of the quilt, ruler aligned with the corner, and begin trimming from there. I use a rotary cutter and slide a cutting mat into place under the layers to make these cuts.

Binding the Quilt

The final step in quilt construction is to sew on the binding. Quilt binding is a continuous length of fabric sewn around the outer edges of the quilt to encase the raw edges. Depending on the color and style of fabric chosen, your binding can create a contrasting, visual frame for the quilt or blend seamlessly with the fabrics it surrounds. The binding step has always been one of my favorites because it represents the final stage of the construction process. Many steps have been completed by the time I arrive at this phase, and the finish is in plain view. At last!

Preferring a narrow binding, I use a 2-inch-wide double fold, straight of grain, continuous binding for my quilts. I machine sew the binding to the front of the quilt, wrap it around the quilt's edge, and hand stitch it to the back. Even though vintage and up-cycled fabric is my go-to for making my quilt tops, I almost always use new, 100-percent cotton quilting fabric for the binding. It ensures a good, stable binding edge and, honestly, with vintage fabric there may be too many little scraps to join together to use in a long length of binding. Here is how I make all of my binding.

DETERMINE THE AMOUNT OF FABRIC NEEDED

1. Add the length of all four sides together and add an extra 10 inches to that number. Divide that number by 42 inches (an average useable width of most quilting cottons) to determine the number of 2-inch-wide strips you will need to cut. Multiply the number of strips by 2 inches. This number is the amount of fabric you will need to create the binding for your quilt. For example, if a quilt measures 50 × 53 inches, 50 + 50 + 53 + 53 = 206 inches. Add 10 extra inches for a total of 216 inches. 216 ÷ 42 inches = 5.14 strips to cut (which should be rounded up to 6 strips). 6 × 2 = 12 inches of fabric. To ensure I have enough fabric for binding this quilt, I would buy ½ yard of 44-inch-wide quilting cotton.

CUT AND JOIN STRIPS

2. To get the number of 2-inch-wide strips you will need, cut across the width of the fabric (selvedge to selvedge), cutting away the selvedge edges. Place the ends of two strips, right sides together, at a right angle to each other under the presser foot of the sewing machine. The bottom strip is laid out to the left of the sewing machine; the top strip should be laid out straight toward your lap. (The strip toward your lap should be on top.) Stitch diagonally across the area where these two strips overlap, from top left to bottom right. Repeat this step to join all the strips together. Trim away all but a ¼-inch seam allowance at each join and press the seams allowances open. Joining them this way, versus just sewing a straight line to join the lengths, allows the bulk of the seam join to be distributed evenly inside the binding when it is folded and sewn to the quilt. (See a.)

a.

FOLD AND PRESS THE BINDING

3. At the ironing board, fold the binding in half lengthwise, wrong sides together, and press. (Tip: I like to roll the binding up as I press, to keep it neat until I use it.)

SEW THE BINDING TO THE QUILT AND JOIN THE BINDING EDGES

4. At the sewing machine, working from the front side of the quilt, position the quilt under the foot midway along one side. Align the raw edge of the binding with the edge of the quilt, starting about 5 inches into the binding length and leaving the first 5 inches unsewn. Begin stitching; use a backstitch to secure, then sew the binding down using a ¼-inch seam allowance. (Tip: It is very helpful to use a walking foot for this step to pull all the layers through evenly, but a patchwork foot will work in a pinch.) Continue sewing until you are ¼ inch away from the corner. At that point, stop, backstitch, and remove the quilt from under the presser foot.

To create a mitered corner, fold the loose binding up and away from the quilt's corner edge, fold it back down again, aligning the raw edges of the binding with the edge of the quilt's second side, and aligning the folded edge with the binding edge you just finished. This fold will create a mitered corner. Begin stitching along the new side, right from the raw edge, and continue until you reach the next corner; repeat the steps to miter the next corner. Continue in this manner for all four sides. Stop stitching 5 inches from the beginning. Backstitch, then remove the quilt from the machine but do not cut away the extra binding.

To join the ends of the binding together, spread the quilt flat on a table with the unsewn edges of the binding facing up and closest to you. (Tip: It is important to have several inches of loose binding on both ends to work with, and very helpful to have your quilt laid out flat before proceeding to the next step.)

Overlap the unsewn binding ends along the edge of the quilt. Measure, mark, and trim the edges so that they overlap by 2 inches. Open the fold of both ends, place the ends right sides together at a 90-degree angle, and pin. Draw a pencil line from edge to edge. Move the quilt to the sewing machine and stitch the binding edges together along this pencil line (see b). Trim the seam allowance to ¼ inch and finger press the seam open. Fold the binding back in half, align the edges to the quilt edge, and finish sewing the binding down.

b.

At the iron, gently press the edges of the binding away from the front. At this point, I like to use quilt clips, clothespins, or something similar to wrap and secure the binding around the edge of the quilt just ahead of where I will be sewing. Using a thin, strong cotton thread that coordinates with the binding color (not the backing color), secure the binding to the back of the quilt using blind stitches spaced about ¼ inch apart. Take advantage of this quiet hand-stitching time by watching your favorite movie or listening to an audiobook.

Note: I have outlined in *Tagged* (page 117) how to create an additional flange trim that is sewn on to the quilt edge just before the binding is added. This is a fun detail to add to any quilt that uses traditional binding.

Quilt Labels

In my opinion, a quilt isn't properly finished until it is labeled. Identifying our work is such an important step in making a quilt, and so often it's overlooked. Don't leave future generations guessing about the details. A simple quilt label can be made from a scrap of fabric and using an acid-free permanent scrapbooking pen to write directly on the scrap. Include the date it was made, the maker, and the person it was made for, as well as any other information you want to include.

c.

To create a basic quilt label, write the information you want to include on a scrap of fabric 3½ × 5½ inches, leaving at least ½ inch or so blank at the edges. Cut a piece of muslin the same size as the label, and place the muslin and the label right sides together. Stitch both pieces together with a ¼-inch seam allowance, around all four sides, leaving an opening of at least 1 inch for turning. Trim the bulk at the corners, and turn the piece right side out, pushing out the corners (see c). Press the label flat, folding in the edges used for turning. Hand sew the label to the back of the quilt at one of the corners, using tiny hem stitches around all four sides.

Quilt labels can be decorative and pretty too! I have included templates for some beautiful labels from some very talented artists (page 165).

Hanging a Quilt

I suggest making some of the quilts in this book as wall hangings. To create a hanging sleeve that will securely hang your finished quilt on the wall, cut a piece of muslin or coordinating fabric that measures 8½ inches wide × the width of your quilt (measured from inside binding edge to inside binding edge) plus 1 inch. So, for a quilt that is 23½ inches wide, my cut muslin piece would be 24½ × 8½ inches. Create a hem on each of the short sides by turning ¼ inch toward the back of the fabric, press, then turn another ¼ inch, press (enclosing the cut edge). Machine stitch these hems with coordinating thread, backstitching at each end.

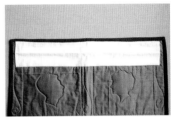

d.

Fold the muslin piece in half, lengthwise, wrong sides together, and press a crease at the fold line to mark. Open the fold, then fold in each of the long cut edges to line up with the marked fold line you just made, wrong sides together. Press those new folds to mark them. Unfold, then refold, wrong sides together, so the two long edges meet. Stitch the two long cut edges together using a ¼-inch seam allowance and press open (try to avoid pressing out the folds already in the sleeve). This seam is on the right side of the fabric, which seems counterintuitive, but it will help everything lay nice and flat on the wall. At this point, if you lay the sleeve on your worktable with the long seam facing down, lining up the fold lines you pressed earlier, you will notice you have a little extra room on the side of the sleeve closest to you. This extra room is important, as it allows a rod or wooden dowel to fit inside without distorting how the quilt hangs on the wall.

Pin the muslin sleeve in place at the top of the back of the quilt, seam side of the sleeve facing down, and hand stitch the sleeve in place with small blind stiches. Be careful to stitch along the press line to not lose the extra hanging room in the sleeve (see d).

Cut a wooden dowel to the width of the quilt plus 1 inch (or use an adjustable curtain rod), so that it extends a bit beyond either side of the quilt. You can use a pretty ribbon tied to each end of the dowel to hang from a single nail or balance the dowel on small tacks or nails.

Templates

Photocopy the templates at the sizes indicated. All templates are also available to download as PDFs at www.wisecrafthandmade.com/templates.

WHOLE CLOTH
(page 29)

Enlarge by 40%

Night,
Night

SPIRIT (page 69)

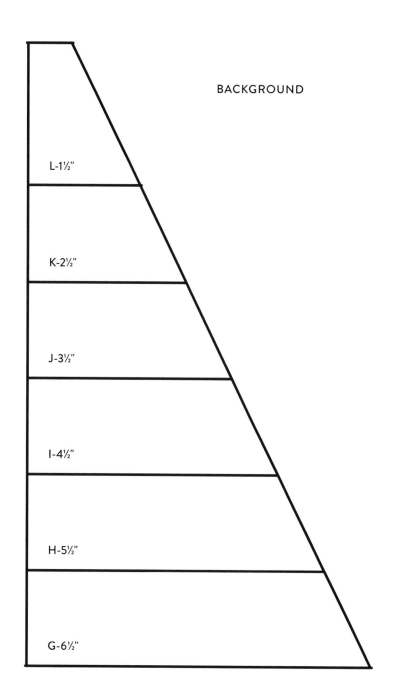

BACKGROUND

L-1½"

K-2½"

J-3½"

I-4½"

H-5½"

G-6½"

Shown at Actual Size

TREE

Shown at Actual Size

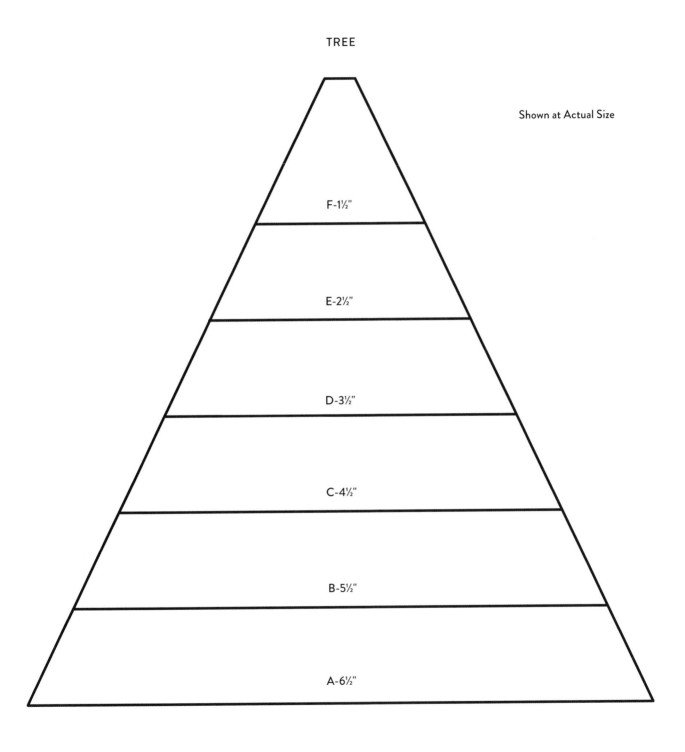

F-1½"

E-2½"

D-3½"

C-4½"

B-5½"

A-6½"

TAUPE (page 85)

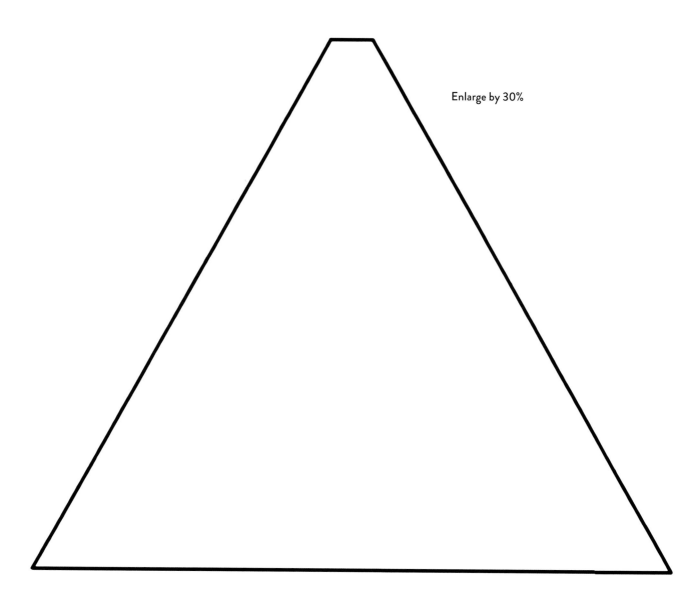

Enlarge by 30%

MUUMUU (page 99)

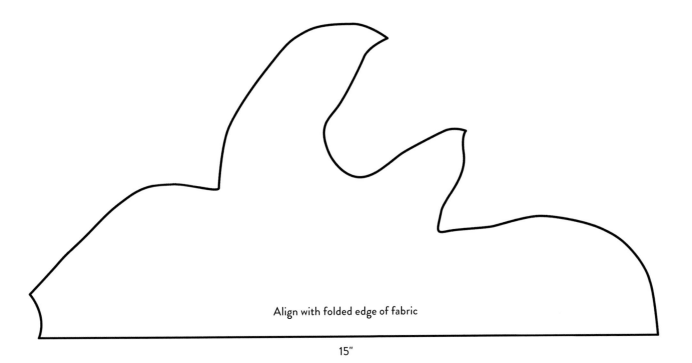

Align with folded edge of fabric

15"

Enlarge by 60%

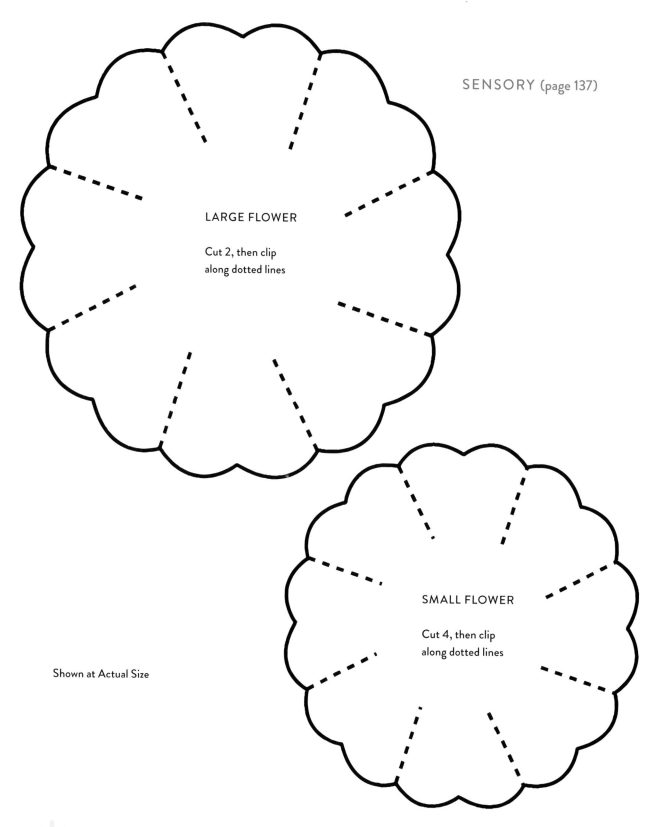

SENSORY (page 137)

LARGE FLOWER

Cut 2, then clip
along dotted lines

SMALL FLOWER

Cut 4, then clip
along dotted lines

Shown at Actual Size

Quilt Labels

Here are some quilt label designs, which can be personalized and sewn onto your quilt. You can either print out your favorites on fabric sheets using your home printer (PDFs of these label are available for download from my website at www.wisecrafthandmade.com/templates) or order fabric printed and ready to be used from my shop, "wisecrafthandmade," on Spoonflower.com (see Resources). These little works of art might be just the thing your special quilt needs.

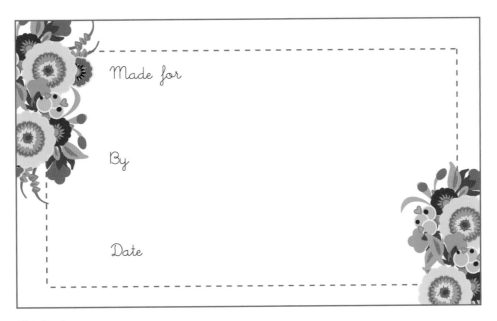

Made for

By

Date

Blair Stocker
wisecrafthandmade.com

Jennifer Stocker
jennystocker.com

made with love
by
for
date

Pam Garrison
pamgarrison.com

this quilt was...

MADE BY :: _____

MADE FOR :: _____

DATE MADE :: _____

Lisa Solomon
LisaSolomon.com

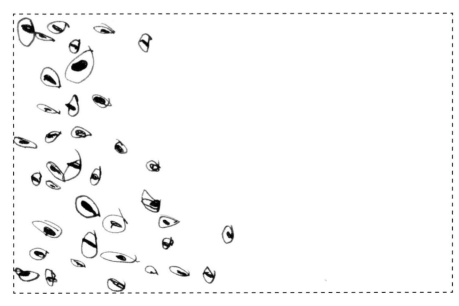

Lari Washburn
lariwashburn.com

Resources

Here is a list of my favorite quilting and sewing supplies and where to find them online. You can find me and more about about my process online at www.wisecrafthandmade.com.

Patchwork and Quilting Tools

Aurifil Threads
www.aurifil.com

Makers of the 50-weight cotton quilting thread I use for all my patchwork and machine quilting

BioKleen
http://biokleenhome.com

Washing soap and spray cleaners for cleaning vintage fabrics

Clover USA
www.clover-usa.com

Marking pens, flower head pins, quilting clips, and leather thimbles

Creative Grids
www.creativegridsusa.com

I used their 60-degree equilateral triangle ruler #CGRT60 for *Taupe* (page 85).

Dharma Trading
www.dharmatrading.com

For the "Blueprints on Fabric" material used for *Cyanotype* (page 125)

DMC Perle Cotton
http://www.dmc-usa.com

Makers of the Perle Cotton Size 8 thread I use for hand quilting

Flatter Smoothing Fabric Spray
http://us.soakwash.com

Wonderful smelling and effective alternative to spray starch

Fusion Beads
www.fusionbeads.com

Where I purchase all my sew-on Swarovski crystals for the embellishment work I do

Hobb's Wool
www.hobbsbatting.com

Maker of the beautiful washable wool batting I used for the *Spirit* (page 69)

Paper Pieces
www.paperpieces.com

Where you can purchase the complete kit of paper templates for *Hand Stitched* (page 105) (search for "Wise Craft Hand Stitched") and the hexagon templates for *D'Orly* (page 53)

Purl Soho
www.purlsoho.com

For a large selection of Liberty of London fabrics, sashiko thread, and needles

Quilter's Dream
www.quiltersdreambatting.com

The supplies of my absolute favorite quilt batting, Quilter's Dream Regal

Quilting Creations Stencils
www.quiltingcreations.com

I used their Clamshell #272 stencil for *Leaving the Nest* (page 93).

Retro Clean
http://retroclean.com/retroclean/

Washing soap to brighten vintage fabrics

Sizzix
www.sizzix.com

I used the Sizzix Big Shot Die Cutter and Equilateral Triangle Die #658663 for *Taupe* (page 85).

Spoonflower
www.spoonflower.com

Make your own custom fabric for *Cameo* (page 131) and order the quilt label designs (page 165) on yardage, ready to use.

The Stencil Company
http://quiltingstencils.com

I used their #ZNC-036-8 Flower Stencil in the *D'Orly* quilt (page 53).

For Secondhand and Vintage Fabric

eBay, www.ebay.com

Etsy, www.etsy.com

Garage Sales

Thrift Stores

Cameo Resources

These sites offer helpful tools and tutorials to create silhouette-type images with your own photos, such as the ones in the *Cameo* quilt (page 131).

Paint.net

Picasa.google.com

Convert-my-image.com

Pixlr.com

PicMonkey.com

Books to Further Inspire Your Quilt Making

The Architecture of the Quilt by William Arnette (Tinwood Books 2002)

Make + Love Quilts: Scrap Quilts for The 21st Century by Mary Katherine Fons (C & T Publishing 2014)

Modern Quilts Traditional Inspiration: 20 New Designs with Historic Roots by Denyse Schmidt (Stewart, Tabori, and Chang 2012)

The Quilters: Women and Domestic Art, an Oral History by Patricia Cooper and Norma Bradley Buferd (Doubleday 1978)

Quilts: Masterworks from the American Folk Art Museum by Elizabeth V. Warren (Rizzoli 2010)

Acknowledgments

I will always remember the period of time during which I wrote this book. I got to wake up each day knowing I was tasked with making patchwork quilts from cherished collections. There are not many things I would rather do. Composing these pages made me a better quilt maker, as did the many people and groups who have supported me along the way. I would like to acknowledge them and let them know how much their support has meant, and continues to mean, to me.

My agent, Alison Fargis (Stonesong), has been a wonderful fan and true supporter of my work, a pro and advocate in every sense. My publisher, Roost, believed in this project and my ability to create it, and working with them has been a dream. Working alongside my editor, Jennifer Urban-Brown, I have felt supported from day one. She gave me freedom to explore my vision of this book, yet guided me brilliantly. Thank you.

To Stephanie Congdon Barnes (http://3191milesapart.com), your photos capture the true soul of what I love about this project. My quilts are meant to be out in the world, used by people who love them and want to see them daily in their homes. I knew the person to visually tell that story would be you. Our collaboration and friendship have been truly inspiring. Your ability to take guidance from my jumbled notes and random texts and make such stunning images is talent personified.

I credit Denyse Schmidt (www.denyseschmidtquilts.com) with inspiring my lifetime love of quilt making. Seeing her quilts all those years ago opened my eyes to a world of patchwork that still inspires me today, and I am forever grateful. Her work and impeccable eye for color and design inspire me to always stretch myself.

Jennifer Stocker (www.jennystocker.com), the very best friend I could ever have, and lucky me to have you as my sister. You are always there to help me work through the moments I'm creatively stuck, have the uncanny ability to see my scattered ideas about things in objective ways, and help me keep true perspective. Thank you for your beautiful work on *Tagged* and the quilt label.

Ahna Holder, I'm so glad we've remained friends all these years. Thank you for sharing your creativity with me and contributing your story to *Sensory*.

Melissa Frantz, you are more awesome than I can describe. Thank you for trusting me with your beautiful dress for *Frock*.

Thank you to Ben Spencer for giving me those cases of salesman sample swatch cards that became *Willy Loman*.

Thank you to Janene McMahan for allowing me to cut into baby Aedan's clothes and create *Baby*.

Katie Pedersen (www.sewkatiedid.wordpress.com), thank you for sending me those fabric squares to make my first value quilt all those years ago. Little did I know I would still be inspired by value all these quilts later.

Thank you to Cathi Bessell-Browne (www.gertrudemade.com) for her support and contribution of the beautiful barkcloth fabrics for *Medallion*.

Thank you to Lisa Solomon, Pamela Garrison, and Lari Washburn for contributing the beautiful quilt labels.

Thank you to Lisa Congdon (www.lisacongdon.com) for allowing her home to be the setting of many of the beautiful photographs within these pages.

To everyone at the Seattle Modern Quilt Guild, thank you for being my people, testing my patterns, and welcoming me in.

To the readers of *Wise Craft Handmade*, thank you for always cheering and supporting my work. Without you, none of this would be possible.

A special thanks for the generous donations of Aurifil Threads, who provided all the sewing thread used in the projects; Quilter's Dream, for providing their wonderful batting; and Retro Clean, for providing cleaners to make my vintage fabrics beautifully clean. Sizzix provided me with the Big Shot Die Cutter and Triangle Die I used for *Taupe* (page 85).

A big thank you to Peter, Emma, and Ian, the people who truly know me (flaws and all), yet love me anyway. Thank you to my extended family, who support my work and feign interest about quilts and crafting even if I ramble on about it, which I often do.

About the Author

A former textile designer and apparel merchandiser, Blair Stocker has been a prolific creative her whole life. She makes modern quilts and home accessories, and is most inspired by vintage, old, and forgotten textiles. She teaches creative reuse, upcycling, and quilt making both in person and online. She lives in Seattle, Washington, and can be found online at wisecrafthandmade .com. This is her second book.